# Romanies in Michigan

DISCOVERING THE PEOPLES OF MICHIGAN

Russell M. Magnaghi, *Series Editor*
Arthur W. Helweg and Linwood H. Cousins, *Founding Editors*

*Ethnicity in Michigan: Issues and People*
Jack Glazier and Arthur W. Helweg

*African Americans in Michigan*
Lewis Walker, Benjamin C. Wilson,
and Linwood H. Cousins

*Albanians in Michigan*
Frances Trix

*Amish in Michigan*
Gertrude Enders Huntington

*Arab Americans in Michigan*
Rosina J. Hassoun

*Asian Indians in Michigan*
Arthur W. Helweg

*Belgians in Michigan*
Bernard A. Cook

*Chaldeans in Michigan*
Mary C. Sengstock

*Copts in Michigan*
Eliot Dickinson

*Cornish in Michigan*
Russell M. Magnaghi

*Danes and Icelanders in Michigan*
Howard L. Nicholson, Anders J. Gillis, and Russell M.
Magnaghi

*Dutch in Michigan*
Larry ten Harmsel

*Finland-Swedes in Michigan*
Mika Roinila

*Finns in Michigan*
Gary Kaunonen

*French in Michigan*
Russell M. Magnaghi

*French Canadians in Michigan*
John P. DuLong

*Germans in Michigan*
Jeremy W. Kilar

*Greeks in Michigan*
Stavros K. Frangos

*Haitians in Michigan*
Michael Largey

*Hmong Americans in Michigan*
Martha Aladjem Bloomfield

*Hungarians in Michigan*
Éva V. Huseby-Darvas

*Irish in Michigan*
Seamus P. Metress and Eileen K. Metress

*Italians in Michigan*
Russell M. Magnaghi

*Jews in Michigan*
Judith Levin Cantor

*Latinos in Michigan*
David A. Badillo

*Latvians in Michigan*
Silvija D. Meja

*Lithuanians in Michigan*
Marius K. Grazulis

*Maltese in Michigan*
Joseph M. Lubig

*Mexicans and Mexican Americans in Michigan*
Rudolph Valier Alvarado and Sonya Yvette Alvarado

*Norwegians in Michigan*
Clifford Davidson

*Poles in Michigan*
Dennis Badaczewski

*Romanies in Michigan*
Martha Aladjem Bloomfield

*Scandinavians in Michigan*
Jeffrey W. Hancks

*Scots in Michigan*
Alan T. Forrester

*Serbians in Michigan*
Paul Lubotina

*Slovenes in Michigan*
James E. Seelye Jr.

*South Slavs in Michigan*
Daniel Cetinich

*Swedes in Michigan*
Rebecca J. Mead

*Yankees in Michigan*
Brian C. Wilson

---

Discovering the Peoples of Michigan is a series of publications examining the state's rich multicultural heritage. The series makes available an interesting, affordable, and varied collection of books that enables students and educated lay readers to explore Michigan's ethnic dynamics. A knowledge of the state's rapidly changing multicultural history has far-reaching implications for human relations, education, public policy, and planning. We believe that Discovering the Peoples of Michigan will enhance understanding of the unique contributions that diverse and often unrecognized communities have made to Michigan's history and culture.

# Romanies in Michigan

*Martha Aladjem Bloomfield*

Michigan State University Press

*East Lansing*

Michigan State University Press
East Lansing, Michigan 48823-5245

Printed and bound in the United States of America.

28  27  26  25  24  23  22  21  20  19      1  2  3  4  5  6  7  8  9  10

LIBRARY OF CONGRESS CATALOGING-IN-PUBLICATION DATA
Names: Bloomfield, Martha Aladjem, author.
Title: Romanies in Michigan / Martha Aladjem Bloomfield.
Description: East Lansing : Michigan State University Press, 2019.
| Series: Discovering the peoples of Michigan | Includes bibliographical references and index.
Identifiers: LCCN 2018059361| ISBN 9781611863406 (pbk. : alk. paper)
| ISBN 9781609176167 (pdf) | ISBN 9781628953794 (epub) | ISBN 9781628963809 (kindle)
Subjects: LCSH: Romanies—Michigan—History. | Romanies—United States—History.
Classification: LCC DX201 .B55 2019 | DDC 305.8914/970774—dc23
LC record available at https://lccn.loc.gov/2018059361

Book and cover design by Charlie Sharp, Sharp Des!gns, East Lansing, MI
Cover photo: Kanalos, Piskor, Lipko, Milanovich, and Ferry families at Lyle Street
Block Party in Delray, Michigan, circa 1948. Courtesy of Casey Kanalos.

Michigan State University Press is a member of the Green Press Initiative and is
committed to developing and encouraging ecologically responsible publishing
practices. For more information about the Green Press Initiative and the use of
recycled paper in book publishing, please visit *www.greenpressinitiative.org*.

Visit Michigan State University Press at *www.msupress.org*

We never lost our heritage inside our skins or our identity even if we were forced to walk away from our heritage in the outside world.

—Angeline Rosemarie M.

To all the Romanies who were courageous and helpful in sharing their voices and stories—their memories, family heritage, history, culture, and challenges with me, a *gadji*, a non-Romani, with hopes that others will shed their fears, speak up, and share their stories so that more *gadjé* may learn about their challenges, accomplishments, and contributions to society to help dispel prejudice and stereotyping—thank you.

In memory of up to one and a half million Romanies whom the Nazis murdered in the Holocaust.

In memory of Burton Myron Leland, retired state senator of Michigan and Wayne County commissioner—a good friend for more than thirty-five years who taught me to appreciate the multifaceted life and diversity of Detroit's many ethnic communities through ongoing conversations and visits.

# Contents

# Foreword

*Ian Hancock*

M artha Bloomfield's book adds further to the recognition of Romani Americans, "Gypsies," a people with whom the general public is far more familiar in story and song. But Romanies in the United States are a very real people, as this book shows, and are quite unlike the storybook Gypsies.

Leaving India a thousand years ago and coming into the west some two centuries later—in each case the result of the eastward and westward spread of Islam—the ancestors of the Romani people brought with them a language and a culture from their ancestral homeland that are still maintained.

It will be clear in this book that the Romani American population is far from monolithic; as in the country as a whole, there are several distinct groups in Michigan. Upon arrival in southeastern Europe, some groups continued to move to the north and west, while others were kept in the Balkans and enslaved because of the demand for their artisan skills, a condition that lasted until abolition in the mid-nineteenth century. Those who reached the northern European coast moved on into Scandinavia, Britain, France, and Spain, while those who followed them remained in central Europe. Separated by time and distance, the various groups acquired differences in the ancestral core culture, and in their dialects of our language, Romani.

As Europe's first "people of color" who were neither Christian nor had a country, their reception was everywhere hostile. Once European colonization overseas began in the fifteenth century, the new territories provided convenient places to which to send their unwanted "Gypsies." The Spanish and the Portuguese were transporting groups of Romanies to their colonies in India, Africa, and the Americas; some were left on a Caribbean island by Christopher Columbus on his third voyage in 1498. The French later sent Romanies to North America and the West Indies, as did the English and Scottish governments. For a brief time, even Sweden had a policy of expulsion during their brief colonization of Delaware (1638–1655).

Most Romani Americans, however, descend from the families who moved out of the Balkans after the abolition of slavery, or from those who were sent here or came here from Britain, or from those who left central Europe following political and religious disruption—all three coming in their greatest numbers during the latter half of the nineteenth century. Others have come since and are listed in this book.

A headache for journalists, the labels applied to the various Romani groups are confusing. Because the early migrants from Asia began to fragment (in what is today Turkey) at the time when the language and ethnicity were crystallizing, there was no single account of "origins" shared by all groups. The Europeans provided the names as they thought fit, the commonest being "Egyptians" (hence "Gypsies," "Gitanos," "Gitans," etc.) or "Tsigani" (hence "Cigan," "Zigeuner," etc.), a Greek word meaning "untouchable."

This last was a reference to Romani culture, which, as in India, places social barriers between various sections of the population. This includes the non-Romani world, kept out as a dangerous and spiritually unhealthy place. This "shield" has in large part helped insulate the Romani people over the centuries from integrating and assimilating. But neither "Egyptian" nor "Tsigani" is the correct label. It is not what we call ourselves when we speak our own language. Each group has its own self-ascription, among them Sinti, Romanichal, Manush, Calé, and Roma. This last has become the PC label of choice, but for most groups it simply means "married Romani men"; Sinti, for example, would never call themselves "Roma" as a group label. When speaking English, then, the fallback word is "Gypsy," despite the fact that it is historically wrong and is routinely applied to populations who have nothing to do with Romanies. We use the word but are uncomfortable hearing others use it.

This book is the result of long and careful research. Martha Bloomfield got to know those whose lives and stories she documents here and has been scrupulously careful to respect identities and to avoid the stereotypes that abound. Describing a very private people, she made new friends, and that is surely a testimony to her sensitivity and scholarship. This could be a book four times its size, and perhaps in due course we will see more from Martha Bloomfield.

# Preface

The purpose of this book is not to tell the whole history of the Romanies (Romas, Roms, "Gypsies") in the world, or the United States, or specifically Michigan. Neither is it to tell of all the different groups of Romanies, or to analyze them, make generalizations, or draw conclusions about their history and stories. My goal is to introduce them by sharing their voices and stories in their own words, from their own perspectives in the greater social and historical context of Michigan history. It is the first book to include oral history interviews of Romanies in the United States and specifically in Michigan.

I refer to these people as Romanies or Roma and not "Gypsy," on the advice of Professor Emeritus Ian Hancock, retired director of The Romani Archives and Documentation Center at the University of Texas at Austin:

> It's true, we [Romanies] use the word "Gypsy" but then we know who it refers to. The objection is to its use by others to refer to other ethnic or social groups (Irish Travellers, chorus-line dancers, retired RV-ers, etc.). It's not so much a slur (for most people) but a mis-application of the word. In a lot of languages, its equivalent (Tsigan, Zigeuner, and so on) is used as an insult. In English, there are other words used as insults, such as gyppo, pikey, and the expression "I got gypped." Etc.

However, many of the people I interviewed preferred the word "Gypsy." I have tried to honor people's requests and preferences. Please forgive me if I inadvertently erred. For direct quotes, I have retained the speaker's or author's use.

In January 2016 I began my journey to discover the Romani history and their people in Michigan. My first challenge was to find books and articles about them in general and then specifically in Michigan. While most resources were about Romanies who lived outside Michigan, many Michigan newspaper articles talked about police "shooing" them out of outlying Michigan communities as early as the late nineteenth century until today. Police reinforced the stereotypes and cautioned people to beware of "Gypsy" scams and theft. While some stories may have been true, mostly *gadjé*, or non-Romanies, wrote about them, giving a skewed, prejudicial perspective.[1] Little other information has been published in Michigan in the past one hundred years.

Other Michigan writers' observations and occasional historic photographs and snippets of interviews from local historical societies and archives were helpful. While these treasures were few, they were gems, as they provided clues and evidence of the Romani presence in Michigan.

As a *gadji*, my second, and perhaps my most important, challenge was to discover Romanies to interview who were willing to share their life stories—memories, family heritage, history, culture, and challenges—through their own voices and roles in Michigan as a marginalized people. By collecting and listening to people's personal stories, we can better understand their history and culture. Unfortunately, Romanies prefer to remain hidden from mainstream society because of extreme prejudice they have experienced all through the years.

Šani Rifati, educator, musician, dancer and founder of the Voice of Roma, wrote, "The Media, written or broadcast, fictional or nonfictional, particularly in Europe, have helped to develop ideas about Romany people, and shaped negative public option about us. But a very curious and sad thing is that, of all the inaccurate and often insulting images of Rroma in the media, none of them originated from Romani sources, and no one ever consulting with Rroma about the truth of what the media portrays."[2]

First, I discovered Steve Balkin, professor emeritus of economics from Roosevelt University in Chicago, who grew up in Delray, an old part of

Detroit. He listened to the Hungarian-Slovak Romani musicians play their music there. He wrote, "I grew up hearing the legend French Gypsy musician Django Reinhardt on the radio and the records, and I needed that as an antidote to depression. Later, I was thrilled to learn that real Gypsies lived and played music in the Detroit area."[3]

He suggested I contact Steve Piskor, author of *Gypsy Violins: Hungarian-Slovak Gypsies in America*, who wrote about these musicians. Some of Piskor's family had emigrated from Slovakia and some lived in Delray. He grew up in Cleveland but spent a lot of time in Delray over the years. He traveled from Cleveland, Ohio, to Dearborn, Michigan, to introduce me to the Hungarian-Slovak Romani community, encouraged me to gather life stories from the aging musicians before their culture completely fades and graciously granted me an interview.

My third challenge was to establish trust with those whom I met. I told the Romanies that I would not tell their stories—they would tell their stories in their own words and voices. I would merely facilitate the opportunity for them to share their stories because I believed it is important for others to learn about them. I would ask them many questions, but mostly to elaborate their initial answers to my questions. I would not pass judgment or critique their stories.

As part of the northern migration in the United States, many immigrants migrated to Detroit to work for Henry Ford and settled in the Delray area—Hungarian-Slovaks were among them. Then Romanies followed the Hungarian immigrants to Michigan to work in factories and to play their music in Hungarian restaurants and bars. Their descendants were the first ones I met. They are not connected to Romanies who traveled in cavalcades through and near Michigan since the early 1900s.

Because of the 1967 Detroit conflict and major industrial pollution, the Hungarian-Slovak Romanies moved out of Delray to Dearborn, Allen Park, Southgate, and other suburbs. Many other ethnic Americans who had originally worked for Ford also left Delray for these same reasons. Delray had about 23,000 residents during its heyday in the 1930s. Today, the U.S. Census estimates that 2,000 remain, but there likely are even fewer.[4]

One family member led me to another or to a friend. I interviewed multigenerational families. I conducted most interviews in person, but also talked via Skype and on the telephone with those who had migrated to Nevada and even Paris for more musical opportunities or to retire. The Hungarian-Slovak Romani stories and history lie at the heart of this book and corroborated my secondary research.

Some of the Romanies performed with famous non-Romani musicians. Their stories shed light on a rich musical history in Michigan and elsewhere. Not all Hungarian-Slovak Romanies were musicians, as some realized early on that they did not have that natural musical talent and pursued other fields. They included a stockbroker, military and fire department retiree, logistics specialist, retired secretary, retired waitress, and caregiver.

I also interviewed people who had known and worked with the Romanies. Some were descendants of Hungarian immigrants; others were not. Sharing their memories painted a fuller historical picture of Romani musicians and the Delray community.

Because of the rich musical and ethnic history of the Hungarian-Slovak Romanies who lived in Delray and other Detroit suburbs, their recollections also reveal a valuable perspective on historical places and contributions to Michigan's history and diverse culture. I have incorporated additional history to add context to the oral histories—to weave the multicolored tapestry more intricately and multidimensionally to provide more meaning.

My fourth difficult challenge was to find other Romanies, not typically musicians or from the Hungarian-Slovak Romani community, whose relatives had originally come from other countries in Europe, and who might possibly—but not necessarily—have once traveled in Michigan in caravan wagons, then in car cavalcades. They had worked as metalsmiths, fortunetellers, carnival workers, horse traders, asphalt road construction workers, roofers, auto repairmen, and office workers. During the course of my research, I asked my friends and people I happened to meet if they knew any Romanies. Most said they were unaware that Romanies even lived in Michigan. Additionally, Romanies often identify with their families' country of origin, which made my search even more difficult. They often do not respond to census questions.[5] However, I was lucky to find a few who either lived in Michigan or nearby who had connections to Michigan.

*Romanies in Michigan* is merely an introduction—an appetizer to their diverse, rich, resilient history in Michigan—based on conversations with Romanies to help in at least some small way to make a dent and to curb the prejudice that has plagued Romanies for years and continues to haunt them.

While I conducted in-depth oral history interviews of Michigan Romanies, I have only included snippets of their stories here about those Romanies who originally came from India hundreds of years ago and traveled to Europe, Latin America, and the United States, and eventually Michigan; I then focus on traditional modes of travel, prejudice, those living in outlying areas of Michigan, their musical community in Delray, and their lives today.

Throughout this book, we will hear different voices. Some represent old perspectives; others represent newer perspectives. Some are in harmony with one another; others are not. In any event, this book presents an opportunity to hear from both the Romanies and *gadjé*. Some Romanies I interviewed talked about their identity, history, thoughts, and challenges with the *gadjé*, and their feelings as a minority: self-efficacy, respect, and pride in their culture and work as they pursue their life goals. They reflect quite a different perspective from those in prejudicial newspaper articles. These multifaceted interviews provide unlimited opportunities to begin to discover and understand these people.

# Acknowledgments

Many friends and colleagues helped me tremendously throughout my journey over several years. Librarians, archivists, and academics recommended books, articles, newspaper stories, and movies and shared archival oral histories as well as opportunities to view artifacts, photographs, and government reports.

Thank you to Steve Balkin, professor emeritus of economics, from Roosevelt University in Chicago, who grew up in Delray, an old part of Detroit, and who suggested I contact Steve Piskor, author of *Gypsy Violins: Hungarian-Slovak Gypsies in America*. Piskor wrote about these musicians, friends, relatives, and ancestors in his book, and introduced me to some of those who had originally lived in Delray. I am grateful for all his help.

Most importantly, I am indebted to all of the people I interviewed in person, by telephone, and on Skype, with follow-up e-mails and messages. I always gave them the opportunity to review their transcriptions, which fostered more trust. The majority of people were from the Hungarian-Slovak Romani community. Interviewees include: Steve Piskor; Elaine Horvath Moise, her son, Victor Moise, and her granddaughter Angeline Moise Malavenda; Richard Margitza, his wife Eleanor Margitza, and their son, Rick Margitza; Billy Rose (stage name for Bill Slepsky), his son Chris Slepsky, his granddaughter Lauren Slepsky-Chicko, and Lauren's maternal grandmother,

Evelyn Horvath Hallup; Don De Andre and his daughter, Renee Andra Bandy; Casey "Geza" Kanalos; and Richard S. Martin.

Thank you, Angeline Rosemarie M., a Michigan Romani woman who courageously shared her family's history, a composite of multiethnic groups, some of whom are Romani and played in the Royal Hungarian Gypsy Band from Galicia, and others who were Travellers from Ireland.

After I fell off the now late thoroughbred chestnut horse Diamond, I wanted to make sure I did not have a concussion so went to the emergency room at Sparrow Hospital in Lansing, Michigan. I was fine and had the good fortune to meet a nurse there who put me in touch with pastor/anthropologist Larry Merino, a Romani, now retired outreach pastor from Holy Cross Lutheran Church in Fort Wayne, Indiana, whom I then interviewed and who provided invaluable perspectives. His family originally came from Mačva in Serbia.

I interviewed Michael Kral, a clinical-community-cultural psychologist and medical anthropologist at Wayne State University who is part Romani and whose relatives came from the Czech Republic; he conducts community-based participatory action research among many groups, including the Romanies in the Czech Republic.

Mandy and Kim Kramar, who raise Gypsy Vanner horses in Charlotte, Michigan, talked to me about their experience of importing these horses from Ireland and then breeding them. They introduced me to David Bryan, whose family were Irish and Welsh Travellers and who now lives in Georgian Bay, Canada. With his wife Christine Bryan, he participated in the Michigan State University Horse Expo in 2017 and 2018 in East Lansing, where I interviewed him.

I also interviewed several non-Romanies who were familiar or who had worked with Romanies who shared their memories: Alex Sagady Jr., environmental consultant; Éva V. Huseby-Darvas, retired anthropologist at the University of Michigan-Dearborn; William Tyler White, owner of White Bros. Music in Bath; Paul Gifford, archivist at the University of Michigan-Flint; and Robert Takacs, who had lived in Delray.

I am thankful to many others who provided advice and encouragement on my long journey. My editor, Russell M. Magnaghi, professor emeritus at Northern Michigan University and editor of the Discovering the Peoples of Michigan Series, shared newspaper articles that dated back to the late 1800s about Romanies, provided me unwavering support as he navigated me on my long journey, and cheered me on from Michigan's Upper Peninsula!

Professor Emeritus Ian Hancock, a Romani, now retired director of the Romani Archives and Documentation Center, the University of Texas at Austin, and foremost scholar of Romani studies nationally and internationally, and advocate for Romani rights, has represented the Romani people at the United Nations and served as a member of the United States Holocaust Memorial Council. He was awarded the lifetime Order of the British Empire by Queen Elizabeth II in 2018. He validated the necessity of my gathering stories directly from Romanies and always answered my never-ending questions. I had the honor to meet him at the Illinois Holocaust Museum and Education Center in Skokie, Illinois, where he talked about the Romanies in the Holocaust.

I am thankful for the support from the board of the Voice of Roma, which, according to its website, "promotes and presents Romani cultural arts and traditions that counters both romanticized and negative 'Gypsy' stereotypes, and contributes to the preservation of Romani identity and culture": Šani Rifati, founder of the Voice of Roma, educator, musician, and dancer who provided insightful comments; Professor Carol Silverman, cultural anthropologist, University of Oregon; and Kristin Raeesi, independent scholar and professional dancer.

I am grateful to Geneva Wiskemann, founder of the Michigan Oral History Association and my loyal friend and mentor for more than twenty years; Chris Dancisak, my good friend and colleague for a quarter of a century, who read and critiqued every word I wrote before anyone else read it and always discussed my half-baked ideas; and Steve Ostrander, friend and coauthor of *The Sweetness of Freedom: Stories of Immigrants*, exhibit designer at the Michigan Historical Museum, and folk and blues musician, who edited some of the complex interviews.

Nancy MacKay, my friend and colleague, encouraged my efforts throughout my journey and validated the necessity of gathering stories from marginalized people. Her career roles as librarian, oral historian, university lecturer, author, editor, and consultant have fed her belief in deep listening and that everyone has a story worth telling. Her enthusiasm rubbed off on me!

Thank you to my friend and colleague, Gail Vander Stoep, associate professor in the Department of Community Sustainability at Michigan State

University, who has always supported my endeavors and invited me to talk to her graduate seminars over the years about the importance of heritage and culture in the lives of individuals and the communities in which they live, their role in identity and community development, and effective strategies for sharing cultural stories and meaning with both local citizens and visiting tourists.

Nancy Besonen, journalist for the *L'Anse Sentinel* newspaper, interviewed me and wrote a beautiful article to help me in my search for Romanies in the Upper Peninsula in Michigan. David Goodman, retired geographer from the Michigan Department of Transportation, who had worked in the Delray area, spent an informative, educational day with me visiting old Delray and the Springwell community in 2017 so I could get a feeling of where the Hungarian-Slovak Romanies had once lived. My friend Bobby Maldonado believed in my endeavors and found a Romani for me to interview. I am grateful to Rachel van Dinkel and Hayley Orzech, who carefully transcribed the oral histories. My friends and colleagues Laura Ashlee and Brian Grinnell, both with the Michigan State Historic Preservation Office, provided useful materials about Delray and the new Gordie Howe International Bridge. Éva Husby-Darvas, retired anthropology professor from the University of Michigan at Dearborn and author of *Hungarians in Michigan* (Michigan State University Press), talked about the Romanies and the Hungarian community.

I visited with the now late William Lockwood, retired anthropology professor from the University of Michigan, who researched the Romanies in the Balkan countries. He donated his scholarly works and documents to the Michigan State University Library.

Other generous people shared their time and knowledge. Kathy Makas, archivist, and Jim Orr, Image Services Specialist, at the Benson Ford Research Center at The Henry Ford, along with other library staff, were extremely helpful. She provided me with a copy of the same photograph of Henry Ford and some Romani musicians that Steve Piskor had also used in his book. She shared transcriptions of several oral history interviews that staff had conducted in the 1950s in which they talked about Henry Ford and Romani musicians.

Others include Deborah Margolis, Anthropology and Middle East Studies librarian, at Michigan State University; Jeremiah Mason, archivist, the Lake Superior Collection Management Center; Jo Orian, oral history technician of the Keweenaw National Historical Park in Calumet; Jessica Harden, archivist, Archives of Michigan; Annakathryn Welch, assistant archivist, Archives of Michigan; Elizabeth Clemens, Walter P. Reuther Library, Wayne State University Library; Terese M. Austin, William L. Clements Library, University of Michigan; Pamela Shermeyer and Michael Brown, the *Detroit News*; Janet Crayne, librarian for Slavic, East European, and Eurasian Studies, University of Michigan; Barry Moreno, Ellis Island, the Bob Hope Memorial Library; Eric Byron, Ellis Island Museum; Dave Curtis, Canton Historical Society; Jan Froggatt, Ferndale Historical Museum; Heather Hames, director, Center Line Public Library; Jon Ringelberg, Clare County Historical Society; Karen Lindquist, Delta County Historical Society; Frank Boles, Central Michigan University, archivist, director of Library; Larry Molloy, president, Keweenaw County Historical Society; Julie Schopieray, research volunteer, Traverse Area Historical Society; Gary Harrington, Ironwood Area Historical Society and the Gogebic Range Genealogical Society; Mackinaw Area Historical Society; Houghton Keweenaw Counties Genealogical Society; Jill Rauh, Reference and Government Information, Benton Harbor Public Library; Dan Truckey, director/curator of the Beaumier Upper Peninsula Heritage Center at Northern Michigan University; Carla Reczek, Dawn Eurich, Joyce Middlebrooks, and Margaret Bruni, Detroit Public Library, Burton Historical Collection; Tobi Voigt, formerly of the Detroit Historical Society, now at the Michigan Historical Center; Jeremy Dimick, Detroit Historical Society; Greg Kowalski, Hamtramck Historical Museum; Richard Bujaki, curator, Old Delray website; Phil Schertzing, Michigan State University School of Criminal Justice; and Lynne Swanson and Pearl Yee Wong, Michigan State University Museum. Others include Michelle Kelso, assistant professor, George Washington University; Professor David J. Nemeth, anthropologist, University of Toledo; Thomas Acton, professor emeritus and visiting professor at Corvinus University, Budapest, and senior research fellow at Bucks New University; William Duna, jazz musician/educator; and Pamela M. Zuber.

I wish to thank Julie Loehr, Michigan State University Press, who provided me the opportunity to write and publish books about immigrants. I also thank Press staff for their help in bringing this book to completion. A special thank you to Anastasia Wraight and Elise Jajuga for their care and patience.

Thank you to everyone who generously shared their photographs with me. Narrowing the photographs down to the ones here in this volume was a challenge.

Thank you to Linda Wallace for her unending support, always believing in my many endeavors and navigating me through all my life challenges for so many years.

I am grateful to my family for their support on my journey—my husband, Alan Bloomfield, my sons Avi Climo and Simi Climo, and my mother-in-law, Betty Bloomfield Soffin.

Please forgive me if I have inadvertently not thanked everyone.

# Who Are the Romanies?

Roma are paradoxically revered as musicians and reviled as people. Under-
lying this phenomenon are dichotomous emotions of fear and admiration.
—Carol Silverman, *Romani Routes, Cultural Politics*
*and Balkan Music in Diaspora*

Who are the Romanies, one of the most persecuted of all minorities
throughout the world? Where did they originate? To where did they
migrate? Why and when did they immigrate to America? Why do they
stay hidden from the mainstream? What is their culture like? How do they
travel? How do they spend their time? Why do people discriminate against
them? Who perpetuates myths and prejudices?

Once we engage in conversation with the "other," it is difficult to maintain
our original prejudice, of which we are all guilty to one extent or another. The
"other" is no longer a number or member of a group but is human just like
each of us, with a unique personality, social identity, and history. Through
discovering and sharing the stories of the Romanies, we can better understand them and share that knowledge to help dissipate discrimination and
prejudice.

Well-known anthropologist Anne H. Sutherland researched and wrote the first major work about the Romanies in the United States in the 1970s: "Partly, the Roma are indisposed to let people know the 'truth' about them as it has been one of their most effective survival mechanisms. A group that is generally despised by those who live around them keeps its boundaries by *not* disseminating full and accurate information. They understandably sense that both inaccurate and accurate information can be harmful to them."[1]

### Romanies Migrate from India to Europe

The origins of the Romanies, as well as their language, lie in northern India. As early as the beginning of the fifth century, they began to migrate to Europe. They first arrived in Ægyptus Minor (Little Egypt) in the western Byzantine Empire while the Ottoman Empire was expanding. People often confuse this with Egypt and erroneously believe that is their country of origin. However, it is possible that some of the Spanish "Gypsies"—the *Gitanos*—passed through Egypt and Northern Africa on their way to Spain.[2] "During their twelve-hundred-year sojourn from India, the Gypsies have endured as landless travelers through the world, subjected to dominant group hostility and violence. Moving from territory to territory, either by desire or force, approximately eight to ten million Gypsies have survived as citizens of the world, living in forty different countries."[3] Linguist Yaron Matras writes: "Their memory of the place of origin might be passed on for one or two generations, but ultimately it is their sense of belonging to a distinct Romani community with its spiritual beliefs and unique practices that defines who they are, not the region their ancestors left behind."[4]

While Europeans initially welcomed Romanies, over time they developed an aversion to them, rejected and persecuted them, and began to hang and/ or banish them. Discrimination, prejudice, and bigotry manifested themselves in a variety of ways and continue today. Ian Hancock writes about some of the anti-Romani laws that were created throughout Europe "to regulate the movement and treatment of Romanies," and the horrors others inflicted on them.[5]

"In Spain, Hungary and colonial Brazil, it was illegal to call oneself a Romani or to speak Romani; in England and Finland, it was illegal even to be born a Romani, in other words, our ancestors were breaking the law simply by existing."[6] Discrimination against the Romanies, many of whom live in extreme poverty, is still prevalent in Europe. And many of these anti-Romani laws were the precursor to early anti-Romani laws in the United States.

During the Holocaust, even before killing Jews, the Nazis rounded up, sterilized, and deported Romanies from all over Europe. They exterminated up to 1.5 million of them. Ironically, on the one hand, the Nazis were killing Romanies—on the other hand, they were listening to their music. "The Gypsies call the Holocaust, *O Porrajamos*, a Romanès, meaning 'The Great Devouring'. . . . When the Gypsies do talk of *O Porrajamos*, their story often begins, 'Music saved my life.'"[7]

### Romanies Come to the United States

During the colonial period, Western European countries dealt with their "Gypsy problem" by sending them to other countries. The Spanish shipped Gypsies to their American colonies (including Spanish Louisiana); the French sent Gypsies to the Antilles; and the Scots, the English, and the Dutch sent them to North America and the Caribbean. Great Britain sent the Romanichal to work as slaves on Southern plantations.[8]

In the 1800s more Romanies immigrated to the United States along with other ethnic groups. Many Hungarian-Slovak Romani musicians went to Braddock, Pennsylvania, outside Pittsburgh, to work in the steel mills. Some also migrated to Cleveland, Chicago, and eventually Delray, Michigan.

Hancock said, "There is thus no homogeneous Romani population but a number of sharply disparate groups differing from others in numbers, in degree of acculturation, and in aspects of their languages and priorities."[9]

### In the United States

Irving Brown, who traveled with the Romanies in Michigan and elsewhere in the United States, said that some immigrated to Latin America from Europe and then migrated to the United States, settling in Chicago. He spent time with those who had lived in Chicago and then migrated to Indiana.[10] According to one young Romani woman with whom I spoke, others frequently went back and forth between Benton Harbor, Michigan, and Chicago.

Newspaper accounts referred to police forcing Romanies out of town, as in the Calumet *Copper Country Evening News*, December 4, 1907: "The gang of gypsies which had been operating in Red Jacket had been ordered out of town, and it is believed the visitors left yesterday afternoon for St. Paul."[11]

By 1980, more than half a million Romanies were living in the United States and Canada. Today, "the largest concentrations of Gypsies are in major urban areas such as Los Angeles, San Francisco, New York, Chicago, Boston, Atlanta, Dallas, Houston, Seattle, and Portland."[12]

Approximately one million Romanies now live in America but remain hidden from mainstream life.

> Their culture too is insular, and intentionally so, to protect what's theirs. Yet in rented dance halls and event centers, for weddings and anniversaries and birthdays and Super Bowl parties across the United States, American Romani are celebrating with their music.[13]

In the 1880s, Romanies began to settle on Cleveland's west side. Within forty years, at least one thousand of them lived in the area known as Ohio City. Romani musicians as well as some nomadic bands who worked as fortunetellers lived there. By the 1970s, the Romani population declined to a few hundred. Some of those migrated to Parma and North Olmsted, Ohio; others went to Delray, Chicago, and New York.[14]

Romanies also followed Hungarian and Serbian immigrants to the Southeast Side of Chicago who worked in the steel mills in the late 1800s until World War I. While the Romanies did not want to work in factories, they created opportunities for themselves to perform music familiar to these immigrants. The Machwaya came from Serbia and parts of the Austro-Hungarian Empire with Serbian populations such as Croatia and Vojvodina. The Kalderash Gypsies also followed Hungarian immigrants to Chicago.[15] Some of the Gypsies living in Chicago also migrated to Delray. In the late nineteenth century, Romani band musicians came from Hungary and performed in the 1893 Chicago World's Fair.[16] They also performed in the Great Lakes Exposition (also known as the World's Fair) in Cleveland in 1936.[17]

Today, the Romanies still migrate across the United States from the Midwest to Nevada, California, Texas, and elsewhere to live close to family and friends or for jobs. Some of those who had once lived in Delray and then in the Dearborn area moved to the Las Vegas area to work or retire. Sometimes they return to Michigan where their friends and family live. When a relative or friend dies or gets married, many Romanies also travel long distances to attend the life-cycle events. Some perform traditional Romani music at these occasions.

## Romani Identity

The Romanies are a huge, complex, diverse group of people who have traveled and continue to travel worldwide. It is not possible to make any succinct generalizations about their beliefs or religious identity globally, specifically, or individually within Michigan. As a means of survival, Romanies are determined not to assimilate into other cultures. This originates from their belief in *marimé* codes "which keep the physical and social contact between the Gypsies and outsiders to a minimum. . . . From the Gypsies' point of view, life within the Gypsy community is safe and secure, while life outside the community is reckless and even dangerous."[18]

Because of their belief system, history of constant migration, and the necessity to adapt to different cultures and societies, the Romanies are amazingly adaptable and resilient, even without a country of their own.

> The American Roma traditionally . . . have a strong sense of identity, an essentialized identity that is rooted in kinship, language, marriage and group practices, as well as timeworn ways of constructing and reproducing negotiations with the outside world. . . . Their ability to negotiate many languages, and different cultures and states, is crucial to how they make their living—by persuasion, fortune-telling and salesmanship.[19]

After experiencing prejudice as a child, Steve Piskor, who grew up in Cleveland researched his identity and ethnic history. He also spent much time in Delray and is familiar with the community who once lived there. He said that as a child, other children would say to him, "'Well you're Gypsy. Well, my father told me there's no such thing as Gypsies and where'd you come from and you don't have a country,' and stuff like that. I couldn't answer the question. So, I went to look for an answer. At that time, I really started the genealogy of them and actually, I didn't know it, but the Cleveland Public Library had the largest collection on the Gypsy people, on Romani people."

Richard S. Martin grew up in Delray, where he went to Holy Cross Church, Redeemer High School, and then Southwestern High School. His father worked for General Motors for about eighteen years in a Cadillac plant and also played in a Romani band on weekends as a lead violinist. When Richard was twenty years old, he married and moved to Riverview, Michigan, where he began working in the logistics industry. After fifty-five years, he retired and moved to the Portage area in Michigan, where his daughter and her family live. He talked about his Romani identity: "My children and grandchildren know they have a Gypsy heritage. However, they also share a Hungarian, Polish, Irish, and Japanese bloodline. . . . As my extended family continues to grow and as time passes, the knowledge of them having Gypsy blood will probably be forgotten."

Casey Kanalos, whose photograph of family and friends appears on the cover to this book, also talked about his Romani identity. His family were "Zemp" Gypsies, who emigrated from Slovakia in the early twentieth century and worked for the steel industry in Bethlehem, Pennsylvania. Around 1929 or 1930 his family moved to Delray to work in the booming automobile industry. His father, Steve Kanalos, was the *primas* violinist, who played in the Steve Kanalos Band.

> I am proud of who I am. I am proud of what my parents had given me and my grandparents. They have given me love. They've given me tradition. Oh, they've given me respect for others. Now, we didn't know much about ethnic groups, where we were raised. To us, we were known as two things: you were either Catholic or Protestant and that was all we knew. . . .
>
> Now we're known as Gypsy. And I know we're trying to get away from that word "Gypsy," but I have to be honest with that area. To me, it would be like spitting on their grave. And everything that they went through in Europe. Everything over there. I am a Gypsy, I don't change. I know they refer to us as Roma, or Romani now, but I'm still a Gypsy and when I say that, people look at me and say, "Ok, you're a Gypsy. What's a Gypsy?"

Musician Billy Rose's granddaughter Lauren Slepsky-Chicko, a contemporary and jazz vocalist in the Metro Detroit area, performs with her grandfather and her father, Chris Slepsky, a multi-instrumentalist whose primary instrument is drums. She talked about growing up as a "Gypsy" in a multiethnic community in the Dearborn area.

Most of the people we went to school with in Dearborn, and in Delray that our parents and grandparents grew up with, knew we were Gypsy. However, you go out into the world today and they're not exposed to our culture, and it's just too foreign for them to understand. If they ask what your ethnicity is, and you tell them, all you hear about are the stereotypes: "Wow, are you a traveler? Are you a fortuneteller?" The other reaction is that they have no idea what it means, and people respond with something such as, "You're a Gypsy? What is that? What do you mean you're a Gypsy, is that a real thing?" ... And once in a while, they just think you're joking or being sarcastic and just laugh and smirk, "Yeah right, you're a Gypsy."

It's just very difficult and frustrating to respond to any of these reactions. How do you explain your whole culture and your whole being in a couple of sentences to someone you've just met? In most instances you feel that you already have to defend yourself that you're a real person, with real morals, and a real culture that explains who you are and that it's not anything like the stereotypes.

Most of us won't say we're Gypsy to the outside world because if we do, we are looked upon and judged differently. All of a sudden, we're so different than we really are, and so different than everyone else. If something goes missing at work or if there is a problem that is not of our own doing, we are the ones who are going to be blamed because all that is in people's minds are the stereotypes.

Šani Rifati, the founder of Voice of Roma, said,

My name is Šani and I am a *Rom*. Rom means human being, or person, or man (Romni is for woman) in the Romany language. ... Being a Rom is not about belonging to a country or a piece of land. It is culture. It is language. It is tradition. It is hundreds of years of oppression, suppression and depression. I am sure that many Rroma can't even come out and say, 'I am a Rom' without fear of repercussions—i.e., people counting their silverware before we leave. I won't play you a sad song on my violin. I do not have a bandanna. I do not have a golden tooth. I do not have long hair or a golden hoop in my ear. I am just trying to speak up for my people: the Rroma.[20]

## Religious Beliefs

Religious affiliations among the Romanies vary and are complicated. Many believe in Romani spirituality. Some are Catholics. Others are Lutherans. Those who have joined the Pentecostal Church are obligated to give up fortunetelling. Some of the Romanies originally from Delray are deeply religious, devout Catholics. Many of them attended the Holy Cross Hungarian Catholic Church as well as the Holy Cross Religious School in Delray.

In 1997 about three thousand Romanies gathered in Rome at St. Peter's Basilica, where Jimenze Malla was beatified "as a martyr to his faith" during a ceremony at which Pope John Paul II presided. Romani violinists performed, and a prayer was read in Romani. Malla had tried to protect a local priest from an anticlerical Republican militia attack when he was seventy-five years old in 1936. "He was held in a former Capuchin monastery, converted into a wartime prison, where he was taunted for his refusal to part with his beloved rosary." He was then killed.[21]

Gypsy spirituality, part of the core culture of Gypsies, derives from Hindu and Zoroastrian concepts of *kintala*—balance and harmony, as between good and evil. When that balance is upset, ancestors send signals to keep people on track. The mysticism of fortune-tellers and tarot readers—though such services to non-Gypsies are not the same as Gypsies' own spirituality—has bases in Gypsy spirituality. Many Gypsies are Christians, with denominational allegiances that reflect their countries of origin. . . .

[M]ost Rom Gypsy Americans are Eastern Orthodox.

Today, around the world, Christian fundamentalist revival movements have been sweeping through Rom, Romnichal, and other groups of Gypsies.[22]

Anne Sutherland wrote about the Romanies in California in her book *Roma: Modern American Gypsies.* She said that since she had studied the American Roma forty-five years before, they have changed in many fundamental ways. The new evangelical or Pentecostal Gypsy churches have trained preachers and focus specifically on the Romanies in Europe and the United States.

> While before they were united through their beliefs and rituals, now they are divided by religion. . . . The church teaches them that they cannot tell fortunes (the Bible says so) and if they steal or cheat *gadjé*, they will be kicked out of the church.[23]

The Romanies have had a diverse, beleaguered history of migration throughout the world and continue to travel today. They often live as a segregated minority with family and friends, as they try to insulate themselves from encounters with tremendous prejudice and ostracism. Even though they have traveled worldwide and live in different communities from one another, they usually keep close ties with family and friends. Some maintain traditional spiritual beliefs while others have branched out to other religions.[24]

Victor Moise, the grandson of the late, well-known Romani cimbalist Gus Horvath, from Delray, said,

> Most kids, I think, would be scared to go to funerals. I'm sure I was originally, but I went to so many that—it was like a wedding. I mean there were thousands of people that would come through on a given night, and it was always very emotional. I think more emotional than non-Gypsy funerals, a lot of grieving, crying, just, I think having the music adds to that sentimentalness. . . . The funeral home where all the Gypsies had their funerals in Delray was Stolichi's. And it was down the street from Holy Cross, so then the morning of the mass, the casket would be carried down the street by the immediate family with the violins and all the musical instruments following it, like procession. I mean that's a very good, good memory.

Well-known guitarist and vocalist Billy Rose, who lived and performed in Delray, said, "Yes, we are all Catholic. We have baptismal records in the Catholic Church at least through the 1800s" from Slovakia and Hungary.

Just across the southern Michigan border, in Fort Wayne, Indiana, is a Romani, retired pastor Larry Merino, also an anthropologist, who headed a Lutheran congregation (Missouri Synod). He talked about his great-grandparents who came from Mačva, in Serbia, and originally settled in San Francisco. Some settled in the San Joaquin Valley in a town called Bakersfield. His family members were fortunetellers and musicians. Others had bakeries and traveled around the United States extensively. Initially, he did not go to school beyond sixth or seventh grade and became a musician and composer. "And so, there I was in my 20s and I was kind of, I guess you would call me a closet Christian. . . . And I couldn't let anybody know, because nobody in the family had ever done this before." Over time, he found people who helped him, and eventually in the 1980s he went to college and moved to Indiana to attend a seminary.

Pastor Merino wrote his PhD dissertation about the "The Machwaya Gypsies in North America who are a resistant people group who use the practice of ostracism to retain group members and to keep the non-Gypsy *gadjé* from penetrating into the culture. The most significant thing about this boundary, from the missiological perspective, is that it has effectively allowed Gypsies to resist the entry of Christian missionaries into the culture and has prevented the spread of the Gospel message among Gypsies in North America."[25]

These short excerpts from in-depth oral history interviews with Romanies reflect varied perspectives on their identity as well as their religious beliefs. They are merely a tiny taste of the rich and varied Romani identity and culture.

# Always Traveling

On the whole . . . travel tends to be seasonal. Roms travel in order to meet
other Roms at annual gatherings and fairs during the spring and summer
months and to explore market opportunities. In the traveling season, travel
takes precedence over commitments such as school attendance. This
makes traveling an important part of the lifestyle and cultural ideology of
many Romani communities. Many Roms who live in permanent dwellings
in houses and apartments keep caravans for use during the spring and summer months.

—Yaron Matras, *I Met Lucky People: The Story of the Romani Gypsies*

The Romanies have traveled perpetually from the time they left India. Traveling has always been a way of life. Without their own country, they have
often had to flee from persecution and discrimination. Once upon a time
they lived in tents and traveled in wagons or *vardos* and actually lived in their
*vardos*. Today, in Europe, they travel by wagon or car. In Michigan, they also
once traveled by wagon but now go by automobile. Law enforcement has constantly tried to stop them from camping, and to quickly "move them along" to
get out of town and the state. However, from a positive perspective, "Life in the
caravan has a meaning beyond mobility. Caravan sites allow related families **11**

to maintain a tight-knit community and to share resources, tools, and even cooking facilities in a way that is not possible in most urban settings."[1]

Ryalla Duffy, whose family still travels by wagon in England, wrote about life in the caravans. She and her family still live in a "bow-top" wagon.

> When Gypsies first traveled in this country, it was with pack ponies to carry the rods and sheets for their tents. As the Gypsies became richer and roadways improved, carts were used. At first, rods were bent over the top of the carts and a rough accommodation top made by covering the rods with sheets. From this, evolved the first Gypsy living waggons. The Romany word is *vardo* and affectionately they are also known as bow-tops or barrel-tops if they are not of the Ledge or Showman's type. . . .
>
> By the mid-nineteenth century, these were frequently seen on English roadsides and the ones in use today have changed very little from the ones in use all those years ago.[2]

> For years Romanies had to move from place to place in order to make a living. Because of this way of life, they lived for hundreds of years in horse-drawn wagons and carts. Although most Romanies have given up the traveling life these days, some continue to travel from town to town in motorized trailers. They still have everything they need inside: beds, tables and chairs, wash basins, cooking equipment, toys, and clothes.[3]

### Historical Evidence of Romanies Camping in Michigan

Early evidence of Romanies camping and traveling in caravans also appears in a few photographs in several Michigan libraries and archives. These particular photographs span the width of the state from Detroit to Muskegon. They include those from Canton, West Detroit, Grand Ledge in south-central Michigan, and along the shore of Lake Michigan on the western side of Michigan.

Someone reported in the *Wayne County Review*, July 2, 1880, that "We were visited by a troop of Gypsies, last week, who had many horses with them. Some of our farmers availed themselves of the opportunity of exchanging horses with them."[4]

*Figure 1. Gypsy Camp. Photo courtesy of the Archives of Michigan.*

*Figure 2. Gypsy Camp near L[ake] Harbor. West Michigan photograph album, 1906–1920. Photo courtesy of Clements Library, University of Michigan.*

More newspaper articles tell us about how the Romanies traveled through Michigan. The *Escanaba Daily Press* reported on July 12, 1929, that "Gypsies in Town, Travel Right Through."

> The gypsies were in Gladstone Thursday but there was no fortune telling. They didn't stay that long. The caravan of big touring cars with the colorful wanderers came from Escanaba, where a short-lived encampment had been made near the ore docks. An escort was in the rear of the procession. In Gladstone, Officer Torval Kallerson assumed the duties of guide, conducting the nomads to the city limits and advising them briefly to be on their way.[5]

### Gypsy Vanner Horses and Caravans (*Vardos*)

In the British Isles, Romanies have favored and bred the Gypsy Vanner horse for pulling their colorful caravan wagons, *vardos*, and for their gentle nature around the Romani campfires and children.[6] Today, the presence of Gypsy Vanner horses in Michigan has impacted the culture and lives of several Michigan horse breeders.

In particular, the owners of WillowWind Stables, Mandy and Kim Kramar, began to breed them after Mandy actually went to Ireland more than twenty years ago, where she bought a few and had them shipped to her farm in Charlotte, Michigan. Meeting the Travellers in Ireland and Wales inspired her to pursue her education first a bachelor's degree in anthropology from Michigan State University and then a master's degree in cultural resource management at Central Michigan University. She wrote about the history of the Gypsy Vanner horse:

> The history of the breed also includes the history of the people. The Travellers of Great Britain and Ireland had the need for a stout, power packed horse that could not only pull a caravan full of their possessions as well as their children, but also be the horse that their children could play with after a long day of traveling. The Traveller's Horse, aka Gypsy Vanner, Gypsy Cob, Irish Cob, was created in Ireland up to 200 yrs [*sic*] ago. The Traveller people would cross heavy pony breeds with the Shire and[/]or Clydesdale. The process of creating [a] 15 hand heavy cob with a small head and ear,

feather, and heavy bone took many decades of skillful breeding. The Travellers horse is exquisite all on its own. The caravan, much like the horse, was a priceless piece of art that was taken care of with love. Each caravan was unique to the family. During the off season, winter usually, the husband would whittle and paint away to make the wagon more detailed, intricate, personal, and more colorful. The caravan was their life's work and they of course took great pride in their work.

Late 2015, we were blessed with the opportunity to have our very own caravan made by a true Traveller, of whom himself was born in a caravan in Wales. Mr. David Bryan built our wagon from scratch while his wife Kristine and their granddaughter Emma painted the wagon with scenes of our own horses. . . . WillowWind Stable has dedicated this caravan to The Bryans and their history.[7]

Mandy said that David Bryan, now in his mid-eighties, met Kristine, a Canadian woman who happened to live in Wales, some years ago. They married and returned to her homeland in Georgian Bay, Canada, northeast of Michigan. David and Kristine visited Mandy and Kim Kramar in the spring of 2017 to see the caravan David had built for the Kramars and their stallion Cheesey, on exhibit at the Michigan State University Horse Expo. While there, David visited with patrons of the Horse Expo and talked about the Romani culture and *vardos*. The two couples now consider themselves family. David and Kristine returned to Michigan in 2018 and participated in the Expo again.

David Byran said,

I am a true Gypsy. I was born in North Wales, one of twins, the other a girl, in a caravan in 1933. My mother was Welsh, and my father was Irish, my grandmother was Irish. All Irish Travellers. We travelled all over Wales, England.

I had to go to London, England, to pass my exams to obtain my license to become a farrier, a metal worker. What happened is, you are going to love this! You got lots of stables on the lawn, on property which belonged to the Queen. It was a park very close to Buckingham Palace. There was stalls set up for about 130 horses. I was there for seventeen days working on all sorts of horses, which had some problems with their feet. They belonged to the Queen. There were twenty-eight blacksmiths who came to get their license.

*Figure 3. David Bryan and his horse Flower, in harness in the bow-top vardo that he built in Halkyn, North Wales, 1982. Flower was classed as a Gypsy Vanner, but there was no registry in those days. She was a Clydesdale crossed with Welsh Cob. Photo courtesy of David and Kristine Bryan.*

You gotta be licensed. Cannot go shoeing without a license. If you do not pass, you are not supposed to do any shoeing. I passed and got my license; so, I am a licensed farrier.[8]

## Impact of Romani Caravans Today

Think about the continuous and increasingly prevalent concept and impact of the "caravan" or wagon on vehicles and homes in the United States and other countries. Today people live, travel, and camp for economic reasons, leisure, and practicality. The vehicles include station wagons, mobile homes, recreational vehicles, and campers.

Vehicle companies use the word "caravan" to promote their product. For example, the Dodge automobile company makes a minivan called the "Dodge Caravan." In Australia, Roma Caravans (which people attach to vehicles) is one of the oldest established caravan manufacturers. "The first

Roma was built in 1928 and we have been building them in Australia ever since. We have many years of caravan building experience."[9]

Additionally, now, tiny houses on wheels have become popular for "financial and emotional freedom, a greener lifestyle, the satisfaction of building one's own refuge. . . . Traditional homeowners are contributing to the trend by building tiny houses on their properties to shelter guests, family members or caregivers, or putting them on vacation land."[10]

Now, people with movable tiny houses encounter similar issues that Romanies have faced (although not prejudicial) with stopping on land that does not belong to them. "Zoning regulations in most places—especially densely developed regions like the New York metro area—typically do not allow full-time living in temporary structures like R.V.s or movable tiny houses. Most tiny homes are built on wheeled trailers that can be towed. Unlike R.V.s, however, tiny houses are generally not wheeled for touring, so much as for flexibility of location."[11]

Today, while Romanies do not usually travel in *vardos* in the United States, some still do in Europe. The wagons served a tremendously profound purpose—as a home and vehicle combined—for a people without a home or country. While Romanies might be more sedentary than they once were, they still travel often to visit family and friends for celebrations, seasonal work, new jobs, or retirement.

# Prejudice and Romanies

As with all legends, that of the Gypsies as thieves has been exaggerated. If they were guilty of all the thefts blamed on them, they would have to travel with moving vans or settle down under the weight of their possessions.

—Jan Yoors, *The Gypsies*

The past and current discriminatory laws, role of the police, negative media, and advertising against the Romanies are extremely complicated depending on when the material was published. This complexity depends on whether laws have changed over time, whether they were state laws or local ordinances, and whether or not cases from one state impacted those of another. Legal issues and the Romanies would be a challenge for law or graduate students, or even seasoned lawyers. The important issue is to acknowledge, share, and begin to understand the problematic, blatant discrimination against Romanies through the myriad ways that it affects their civil and human rights of residency, work, and freedom of speech. The following is a presentation of prejudicial voices, but not an analysis of the subject in the context of this introductory book, *Romanies in Michigan*. Voices come from the media, the police, the legal world, and advertisements—in contrast to the Romani voices from whom we will also hear later.

*Figure 4. A sign displayed in Escanaba Tourist Park (South Park) in Michigan's Upper Peninsula restricts Gypsies and peddlers from camping out, reflecting blatant discrimination. Photo courtesy of Delta County Historical Society, circa 1930s.*

Multidimensional anti-Romani sentiments, which have evolved into the modern-day concept of "racial profiling," originated in Europe many years ago. Romanies have experienced discrimination with regard to residency, employment opportunities, and civil rights—often presumed guilty of some theft and convicted in the press without any legal representation or due process. They have been singled out for labor discrimination as a result of prejudicial advertisements for work at fairs. They have also experienced infringement of their First Amendment right of Freedom of Speech.

Journalists, the police, laws, advertisements, and other accounts have stereotyped and discriminated against the Romanies socially, politically, and economically because of their ethnicity and culture. Laws have reinforced degrading stereotypes of the Romanies and legalized discrimination against them, thus perpetuating misrepresentation and ignorance and white mainstream society's racial dominance.[1]

Persecuted with various degrees of harshness throughout the last millennium during their movement west from Northern India, they have been vilified, subject to laws targeting their traveling ways, forcibly evicted from towns (England, France, US), expelled en masse from the state (present-day

Germany, Italy, and France), enslaved (Romania), imprisoned and exterminated (Hitler's Germany), and forced to settle (Soviet Union and Eastern bloc states). Some have stayed in one place (the Spanish Kale and Romanian Roma being prominent examples), but many have continued to pursue a traveling life and culture based on large kin groups moving round in pursuit of a living.[2]

In the 1930s "Gypsies" were not allowed to camp in some county parks in Michigan. Karen Lindquist, Delta County Historical Society, said, "I do remember that there were groups who came through in my childhood, and I've seen notices warning residents of Gypsies in the early newspapers."

The following words accompanied a photograph in the archives of the Delta County Historical Society in Michigan's Upper Peninsula: "ESCANABA TOURIST PARK—1 mi. so. of bus. district on M-35; 25 (cents) per car; 50 (cents) week per car. Meter charge for trailers. Caretaker."

> South Park had been a privately owned park on Little Bay de Noc of Lake Michigan, with dance pavilion, baseball park, refreshment stands, etc. in the late 19th and early 20th centuries. By the 1930s it had fallen on hard times due to the building of a local city park that was free and located right in the residential part of the city; hence, the use as a tourist park by the 1930s. We really do not know who owned the park by the time of the photo, but it probably was not the city.[3]

In the 1980s, while Romanies camped at a Michigan campground around Battle Creek, they experienced segregation and discrimination, according to Sandra Ballman-Burke, who had also stopped with her husband to camp while on vacation. Quite by chance, they discovered the Romanies, and she wrote about them in her honors thesis, "Gypsies: A Forgotten People." She said that while the Romanies were allowed to camp there, the park officials and other campers treated them poorly. The following is an excerpt from an extensive, detailed description of how badly the park rangers and tourists treated the Romani campers.

> My conversation with other campers usually focused on the Gypsies. Characterizations of the Rom were consistently derogatory. Campground

employees and campers, with one exception, described the Gypsies as dirty. Observation did not support this. Gypsy campsites were neat and clean. . . .

Custodians did not come to clean the bathrooms either the first or second day of our stay. The shower stalls, sinks, and floors were very dirty. Complaints to the park manager accomplished nothing. He insisted that the bathrooms were always cleaned twice daily, "but with these dirty Gypsies here, we just can't keep them clean." The facilities were cleaned a total of five times in twenty-nine days. . . . [4]

## Stereotyping

While many books about the Romanies have been written in an effort to understand them and share knowledge about their lives, rarely does the media portray the Romanies positively. In general, people have very little or no knowledge of them and do not know that they even live or have lived in Michigan. Rather than offering help, hospitality, consideration, or food, the non-Romanies, the *gadjé*, have avoided the Romanies and tried to drive them from their communities. For more than a century, Michigan newspaper articles revealed this anti-Romani sentiment. In Hancock's book *The Pariah Syndrome*, he shared numerous prejudiced cartoons from British and American newspaper headlines.[5] This phenomenon explains, in part, why the Romanies have often opted to remain hidden from mainstream society. "They [the Roma] are accustomed to discrimination stereotyping by those who either exoticize them as free spirits or denigrate them as contemptible thieves. Neither stereotype is accurate."[6]

Ironically, the Romanies also stereotype the non-Romani or *gadjé*:

> While many Americans visit a fortuneteller just once in a lifetime, on a lark, many others seek the advice of fortunetellers on a regular basis. . . . Based on what the fortunetellers hear in their parlors, it is difficult to convince them that there are non-Gypsies who do not commit incest, adultery, homicide, unethical business practices, or a myriad of other antisocial behaviors.[7]

## Media Voices

As early as the beginning of the twentieth century, newspaper articles talk about police whisking Romanies along in Michigan, in both the Upper and Lower Peninsulas, to keep them from stopping in towns and villages, pushing them to leave the state and go to Wisconsin, Indiana, Ohio, and Canada. The *gadjé* have often failed to recognize or appreciate in any positive way why the Romanies constantly travel. They only regard their nomadism negatively.[8] However,

> Roma have been indispensable suppliers of diverse services to non-Roma, notably music, entertainment, fortune telling, metalworking, horse dealing, wood working, sieve making, basket weaving, comb making, and seasonal agricultural work. Many of these traders required nomadism or seasonal travel, and sometimes occupations were combined out of economic necessity.[9]

Negative imagery about the Romanies has appeared in *"gadjé"* newspaper articles. As far back as the early 1900s, Michigan news articles about the Vlax Roma from Southeastern Europe and the Romanichal Romani (originally from the British Isles), who traversed both the Upper and Lower Peninsulas of Michigan, reflect negatively.[10]

> "Drive Gypsies from Village, Fowlerville Marshal Succeeds in Getting Rid of Objectionable Band," special to the *State Journal*, Fowlerville, May 12, 1913

> A band of gipsy [*sic*] horse traders drove into town Saturday morning and made themselves obnoxious about the streets and business places. They were ordered to leave town by Marshall Allbright. An altercation ensued, and the officer threated them with a sojourn in the village lock-up and started off with one of the men. The female portion of the gang interfered and for a few minutes a tug of war ensued between the belligerent parties and in the mix-up the man in question had his clothing nearly stripped off. After a short parley the band finally consented to leave and headed their teams for the west without further trouble. They were a hard-looking lot.[11]

"Gypsies in Town, Travel Right Through,"
*Escanaba Daily Press*, July 12, 1929

The gypsies were in Gladstone Thursday but there was no fortune telling. They didn't stay that long.

The caravan of big touring cars with the colorful wanderers came from Escanaba, where a short-lived encampment had been made near the ore docks. An escort was in the rear of the procession.

In Gladstone Officer Torval Kallerson assumed the duties of guide, conducting the nomads to the city limits and advising them briefly to be on their way.[12]

"Gypsies Turned Loose by Police, No Evidence,"
*Ironwood Daily Globe*, August 28, 1974

Grand Haven, MI (AP). A band of Yugoslavian gypsies even the federal government cannot get rid of is on the loose again.

State Police had to release 34 members of the band Tuesday for lack of evidence after holding them nearly two days while probing thefts Sunday in which nearly $5,000 was taken. Immigration and Naturalization Services officials in Detroit and Chicago described the band, as a persistent headache for law enforcement agencies ever since they entered the country illegally from Mexico sometime this spring.

"They've all been ordered deported," said a government spokesman.

The problem confronting the federal government is finding another country willing to accept the gypsies. So far, no one has agreed to take them.

"Until we do, we're stuck with them. That's the way the law reads," one immigration official said. He conceded that if no other country will take the gypsies, they may stay in the United States indefinitely. . . .

The band first came to the attention of immigration officials late this spring in Arizona. The gypsies said they had been in Mexico City after flying there when they were deported from the Netherlands earlier in the year.

State police picked up the gypsies near Nunica on Sunday night after receiving reports that similarly clad persons had stolen money from unlocked safes or cash resisters at two restaurants near Holland and a sporting goods store outside South Haven.

But troopers were unable to find any loot in possession, of the six women, three men and 15 children.[13]

## Police Enforce Anti-Romani Laws

For years, problems have existed between the police and the Romanies all over the world. While the police accuse Romanies of crimes, the police are also guilty of racial profiling.

> There are a number of police detectives or former detectives who consider themselves to be experts on a special category of what they call "Gypsy crimes." They have been very prejudicial in pursuing so-called Gypsy crimes and tend to believe that most Roma are criminals.[14]

> Law enforcement officers who focus on the people they refer to as "Gypsies" and on "Gypsy crime" are in violation of the constitutional protection afforded Romani Americans ("Gypsies"), who are shielded as a group from this kind of discrimination under the terms of Title VII of the 1964 Civil Rights Act. While an individual must be judged on the nature of this offense, he cannot pay a price for being what he is, though it is abundantly clear that in the United States today, as in the 18th century England, simply being a Gypsy is enough to brand a person as a lawbreaker.[15]

As of 1975,

> The policy of driving Gypsies away, however, is still actively upheld by the American legal system. The June 1975 issue of The Police Chief ("Official Publication of the International Association of Chiefs of Police") contained the recommendation that "Strict laws and the enforcement of them will deter Gypsies from inhabiting your community. The laxness of the laws in a certain area . . . will attract Gypsies. Only in this way can you protect your community."[16]

According to the *Detroit Free Press* staff writer Patricia Chargot,

> Detective Sergeant William Bradway (now retired), Michigan State Police

Detective, was chairman of the Michigan State Police Gypsy Criminal Activity Task Force. He said, "We're just starting to see the real travelers come back." . . . He said that a "gypsy" is a "wandering group of people whose main reason to live is to steal." . . .

Bradway warned against the five most common schemes: "Store diversion. . . . Home Invasion. . . . Utility rebate. . . . Home repair schemes and fortune tellers.". . .

Although no weapons have been used in such crimes, in Michigan, the "younger generation is getting more physical and we expect more violence," Bradway said.

"Gypsies are probably better organized than the Mafia," he said.[17]

The Romanies travel to Michigan from the south to find seasonal outside work. In a fairly recent article on December 13, 2016, in *The State*, a newspaper in South Carolina, Cynthia Roldan writes about an indictment of "Travelers in Murphy Village," but also talks about the local people's respect for the Travelers.

The North Augusta community, just past Interstate 20 in Aiken County, is home to one of the largest communities of Irish Travelers in the nation. According to the 2010 Census, about 1,400 Travelers live in Murphy Village. National counts of Travelers range between 10,000 and 40,000. . . .

On Tuesday, a federal grand jury returned an indictment of 45 counts against 22 people, most of them Travelers living in Murphy Village. The indictment alleges the group committed different kinds of fraud and money laundering schemes, among other charges.

Similar allegations have been raised against Travelers in the past. But for the most part, they are praised within their community in Aiken County. According to published reports, it's common practice for travelers to not target residents in their own neighborhood.

Locals say most Travelers are honest, hard-working people whose reputations have been tainted by the actions of a few. Because they live together and keep to themselves, suspicion of them is rampant. They own lavish homes and mansions in Murphy Village that show few signs of life. The windows of most homes are covered from top to bottom with blinders or are tinted.[18]

## Discriminatory Laws in the United States

Several states, including Pennsylvania, Indiana, Georgia, and New Jersey, passed discriminatory laws that specifically targeted Romani residents, by decreeing it "unlawful for any band of Gypsies . . . to camp in tent, wagon, or otherwise, on any public highway in state" or for it to be "illegal to be a Gypsy without a license." Many of these cases illustrate government officials' and police departments' policies of deliberate harassment, mainly on the basis of Romani illiteracy, since licensing or any documentation requires more than basic reading ability. This tactic serves not only as a means to curtail Romani business interests but also to disregard Romani oral legal traditions and can be considered a further illustration of anti-Romanism in American society.[19]

The following are examples of anti-Romani laws in several states, including Michigan.

In the territory that once was Virginia and West Virginia, Gypsies were legally excluded from the practice of telling fortunes. . . .

The law was not repealed in the state of Virginia until 1930. The new law removed the "anti-gypsy" clause, making Gypsies equal with anyone else seeking a license to engage in fortunetelling, clairvoyance, palmistry, or phrenology.[20]

It is illegal in Pennsylvania to be a Gypsy without a license. . . . Any gypsy who insists on being what he was born—a Gypsy—without a license is liable to up to $100 fine and 30 days in jail. . . .[21]

Gypsies [in the state of Maryland] must pay jurisdictions a license fee of $1,000 before settling or doing business. When any gypsy is arrested, all his property and all the property of members of any groups with which he may be traveling can be confiscated and sold to pay any fine a court may levy against the arrested gypsy. Sheriffs are paid $10 a bounty for any gypsy they arrest who pays the $1,000 fee after he is arrested (Logan, 1976).[22]

Michigan has had its share of anti-Romani sentiment and laws at the state and local levels. Some Michigan state laws include the following: volume 3 of

*The Compiled Laws of the State of Michigan, 1915* describes "An act to prohibit the practice of palmistry, clairvoyancy, astrology or fortune telling by cards or other devices for money or gain, and to provide a penalty for violation of the provisions of this act."[23]

According to an article in the *Los Angeles Times*, "Weather forecasters, stock analysts and even fortune cookies may violate a Michigan law against fortunetelling, says a legislator who introduced a bill to repeal the ban. State Rep. Dick Allen is aiming at a 1913 law that makes people who charge for attempting to foretell the future subject to a misdemeanor. He says the law infringes on First Amendment rights. Violators could be sentenced to 90 days in jail and a $100 fine."[24]

In Otsego, an ordinance "Miscellaneous Offences" does not allow a person "to tell or pretend to tell fortunes by person, machine or otherwise for his gain, reward or profit, the other by means of cards, tokens, trances, inspection of the hands or skull, mind reading, consulting the movements of the heavenly bodies or otherwise." Otsego first passed this ordinance on May 1, 1916. Similar ordinances were passed in Plainwell, Allegan, and Kola.[25]

"Can't Feel Skulls to Learn Future,"
*Lansing State Journal*, Tuesday, April 22, 1930

Phrenology was made a thing of the past in Lansing, so far as public places are concerned, when the city council Monday night passed an ordinance forbidding it. The penalty is a fine of $100 or 90 days in jail.

The police department has had considerable difficulty in the past with phrenologists here, generally gypsies, and the ordinance was passed at the request of Chief Alfred Seymour, of the police department.[26]

"A Court Battle over Fortune-telling is in the Cards . . . Michigan Law:
Banning Fortune Telling for Profit," *Detroit Free Press*, March 29, 1981

Fortune telling by cards, etc., for gain—Any person who shall pretend for money or gain, to predict events by cards, tokens, trances, the inspection of hands or the conformation of the skull of any person, mindreading so-called or by consulting the movements of the heavenly bodies shall be guilty of a misdemeanor.[27]

## Advertisements Perpetuate Labor Discrimination

Another venue for racial profiling in the media was through *The Billboard*, a national weekly entertainment news magazine, founded in 1894. In the past, it had advertisements seeking people interested in performing in circuses, burlesque shows, fairs, and the music industry, including records, radio, and the jukebox. Advertisements promoted fairs, seeking performers for them. It first came out a year after the Ferris wheel appeared at the Chicago World's Fair. It was originally created to cover the "outdoor advertising industry (as well as live entertainment like circuses and fairs. . . . *Billboard*'s main areas of coverage changed over the years to include vaudeville, minstrel shows, motion pictures and recorded music, as well as jukeboxes, radio and, in the 1950s and early 1960s, television."[28]

In the mid-twentieth century, *The Billboard* included numerous stipulations in their advertisements, such as as *No Gypsies, No Drunks, No Mitt Camps, No Flats, No Grift*. They clearly imply that the advertisers are stating that Romanies are deceitful by their very ethnicity. This negative characterization clearly fits the definition of racial profiling and discrimination, perpetuating stereotyping and prejudice.

The Carney Lingo website defines some of the terminology that the advertisements used. Some examples include:

*Mitt Camp*—A fortune telling booth ( . . . from "mitt," slang for "hand," read by a palmist). Being alone with a fortune-teller makes a number of scams possible, from "Your money is cursed, wrap it in this cloth so I can bless it" (you'll never see it again). . . .

*Flat Store* or *Flat Joint* as a game at which the agency has total control over winning or losing. Usually a game at which money is the prize rather than the goods. So called because the "wheel of fortune" or whatever rig is played there, once set vertically for all to see, is not set flat horizontally so that only the player and the agent can see it. After you lose a bunch of money, they might throw you some minor prize to get rid of you. . . .

*Grifters* as a mainstream word from the early 20th century, describing any scam artist. The crooked game operators, short change artists, clothesline robbers, shoplifters ("merchandise boosters"), pickpockets and all other types of criminals associated with some carnivals.[29]

The following advertisements from *The Billboard* also reflect prejudice and discrimination against the Romanies throughout Michigan's Upper and Lower Peninsulas and reveal sponsoring organizations that approved of the discrimination.

Bad Axe

*The Billboard*, The World's Foremost Amusement Weekly Announcements, April 16, 1949:

WANT RIDES, CARNIVAL

No Grift—No Gypsies, For one of the most outstanding celebrations in Michigan. Four-day event. $1,000 worth of fireworks every nite—high act— queen contest. Stage-Free Attractions twice Daily. Sponsored by one of the most active clubs in the state of Michigan. "Bean County Pioneer Days Celebration" Huron County Fairgrounds—Bad Axe, Mich. Sponsored by the Bad Axe Lion's Club, Ray Stecker, General Director, Member Michigan Showmen's Assn. and Showmen's League of America.[30]

Fowlerville and Crosswell

*The Billboard*, July 22, 1950, p. 75 advertisement says, "No Drunks or Gypsies."[31]

Reed City

*The Billboard*, July 22, 1950, p. 75 advertisement says, "No Girl Shows, Flats or Gypsies."[32]

However, not all "want" advertisements in *The Billboard* restricted Romani from applying to work at the fairs. For example, on August 13, 1955, in Mason, Michigan, the advertisement did not include any reference to "Gypsies."[33]

Today, language in announcements for people to work at fairs restricts certain behaviors but not particular ethnic groups. For example, in an online vendor application for the Otsego County Fair in Michigan, the language refers to exhibitors' activities and behaviors, but not the people themselves:

Exhibitors and its employees will not permit or engage in any activity that has potential harm to the health, safety, and welfare of all the people attending the Fair and will not permit or engage in any illegal activity on the fairgrounds.

Exhibitors will be asked to remove any item/items (guns, knives, smut, etc.) that is not appropriate.[34]

The information in these various publications, laws, and advertisements reflect a complex web of anti-Romani sentiment for more than one hundred years from those who reinforce discrimination—journalists, police, the government, and advertisers—in Michigan. It is an extremely narrow, negative view of a multidimensional culture of people with profound history, depth, and variation. These many forums and proponents of discrimination have clearly cultivated and perpetuated a devastating stereotype of the Romanies. They typify others elsewhere in the United States and Europe, wherever Romanies live.

# Romanies in Outlying Michigan

What is it in Roma culture that makes them able to survive in spite of leaving India over hundreds of years previously, moving across the globe, always living within another nation through massive cultural changes from the middle ages to modern times?

—Anne H. Sutherland, *Roma: Modern American Gypsies*

omanies traveling near and through the Upper and Lower Peninsulas in Michigan for more than one hundred years have a history behind them. Some came directly from Eastern and Central Europe to the United States. Others traveled from Europe to South America and Central America and then migrated to the United States. However, this unusual collection of information from a variety of sources paints an eclectic, but not necessarily cohesive, mural of the Romani presence in Michigan.

Non-Romani or *gadjé* writers have portrayed scenes of Romanies camping as well as their rites of passage and musical performances in newspaper articles in the outlying regions of Michigan since the late 1800s. The Romanies were always traveling—as far west and south as Benton Harbor, Michigan, crossing the border into Indiana and on to Illinois, all the way north to Sault Ste. Marie and crossing into Canada, to the western Upper Peninsula crossing into Wisconsin, and as far east as Canton and Detroit and across the border into Windsor, Canada.

Many Romanies traveled in horse-and-wagon caravans and later in large automobiles in these outlying areas. They worked as horse traders, carnival workers, fortunetellers, roofers, and used-car salesmen. Today, they are moving into other professions. Since Romanies have predominantly kept to themselves, "hidden" from the larger communities, it has been difficult to find them to interview. Unfortunately, few primary resources from Romani voices in outlying Michigan are available.

Some who lived in Michigan descended from the "Sigeyner" Romanies whom the Germans shipped to America in the 1800s; their descendants eventually worked for Ore-Ida Foods, the "leading retail brand of frozen potato products in the United States and the world's largest processor of diversified frozen foods."[1]

The women also worked in factories in the Flint area, making weapons for American soldiers during World War II. As welders, they worked on the main gun turrets, which were critical for the survival of the tank and crew and were checked by X-ray for voids or bubbles. According to Ian Hancock, their participation was an important part of Michigan history.

The Hungarian-Slovak Romani musicians and their families who lived in Delray in the Detroit area in the early 1900s are a completely different group of Romanies—culturally, socially, and historically. Hungarian-Slovak Romani families originally followed Hungarian and Slovakian immigrants to Braddock, Pennsylvania; Cleveland; and Chicago to work in steel mills and other factories and to perform music in Hungarian restaurants and bars. Many Hungarians then migrated to Delray, Michigan, to work in Henry Ford's automobile factories for a higher wage. Romanies followed them not only to work in factories but also to perform music in Hungarian restaurants and bars.

### Early Evidence of Romanies in Outlying Michigan

Newspaper articles and diaries reflect early evidence of Romanies in outlying Michigan. While newspaper articles about Romanies appeared throughout Michigan's Upper Peninsula as far north as Calumet in the late 1800s and early 1900s, such articles also were published about Romanies camping in

Michigan's urban and county parks, along the shores of Lake Michigan as far south as Benton Harbor, and in the eastern part of the state in the Lower Peninsula. The articles and excerpts from memoirs are clues that Romanies traveled all over Michigan. Articles also told about life in the various communities where they traveled or camped and about other peoples' thoughts, which often reflected negative, judgmental, and/or ignorant attitudes.

While journalists in Michigan wrote articles in 1899 about Romanies traveling across the state and police pushing them out of their communities and Michigan altogether, similar articles continued to appear in Michigan newspapers well into the twentieth century and even the twenty-first century. Little information is available about where these Romanies came from and where they were going after police and communities drove them out of the state. In some cases, they went to Indiana, Wisconsin, Minnesota, and Canada. For example, "Gypsies crossed on the ferry from the US to Canada; Canadian immigration officials were astonished that the gypsies had about $10,000 in gold. They were heading to western Canada to take up land."[2]

## The Upper Peninsula

Some people have shared brief memories about Romanies traveling through their communities. Daniel Truckey, director/curator of the Beaumier Upper Peninsula Heritage Center at Northern Michigan University, said that he remembers as a kid growing up in Wakefield, Michigan (in the western Upper Peninsula), that

> Every year a "band of Gypsies" would descend on our local campground and stay for a week or more. We were warned not to go down there, or they might steal us. Also, I know that they received very strong scrutiny whenever they entered any store or establishment. I remember that one family had a baby bear cub in a cage, which really did not like it very much and made an awful sound. That's about the limits of my memory about the Romani visits to Wakefield.[3]

John Buckett and his wife, Eleanor, who was born on April 30, 1913, grew up in the Calumet area. Eleanor talked about her memories of Romanies.

"You were afraid they'd kidnap you. That's what you were. . . . They came from Europe and they usually kidnapped kids and sell them."[4]

Local people not only scorned the Romanies, but also looked at them as a spectacle. One article referred to the colorful costumes they wore. However, these were their regular, daily clothes and they were not dressing up to perform in the theater for others.

Barbara Buckett Leary's grandfather, James Trelore Buckett, wrote in his diary about going to see the Romanies in Calumet where he lived.

> Tuesday, April 17, 1906: Went to town and met B. Ban. On 7:30 Lake Linden car. Took her to see German Gypsy played by Al Wilson. Sat in 3rd row of parquetted circle. Went to Lake Linden after theatre and saw B. Ban. Home. Came home on last car at 12:15. Gypsies arrived today and located on ground near Lake Road Yellow Jacket.
>
> Wednesday, April 18, 1906: Arrived home at 1:30 a.m., went to bed. Got up at 6:15 a.m. Fair and very warm all day with rain and colder at night. Went down to see the Gypsies with Bert Kline. Came home and went to bed at 8:30 p.m.[5]

Articles in the *Copper County Evening News* also revealed the Romani presence in the Upper Peninsula. In the following article from 1899, did anyone actually ask the fortuneteller or her husband from where she came? Is the journalist making assumptions? In an article in 1906, the Romanies were convicted in the press. In a second article from 1906, they transgressed an ordinance and were evicted from the community. In a 1909 article, people look at the Romanies as if they are on exhibit.

*Copper Country Evening News*, Calumet, September 15, 1899

The only family of gypsies ever seen in this city are now in camp at Florida on the Lake Linden road opposite Louis Lamorann's store. It is quite a curiosity for the people here to visit the gypsy camp and see how they live and make their home in their hastily constructed camp. The lady is a great fortuneteller and the head of the family makes a living by trading horses. The fortuneteller comes from Egypt and her husband is an Englishman.

*Copper Country Evening News*, Calumet, May 5, 1906

It will be remembered that a week or so ago a band of gypsies arrived in Calumet and located at Tamarack No. 5 location. Matters were made very warm for the band, reports being circulated that the gypsies had fleeced some of the local residents of hard-earned cash on a previous visit. "Once hit, twice shy," went this time, and the gypsies had to hike without doing any "business."

Previous to going they called down vengeance on Calumet and predicted the township would be visited by an earthquake. This report was circulated around town, and a number of local residents went to the Portage Lake towns in the hope that if Calumet was visited with an earthquake, they would be safe. They returned home last evening with the laugh on them.

*Copper Country Evening News*, Calumet, November 13, 1906

Three gypsies, names unpronounceable, were arrested yesterday afternoon and brought before Justice Jackola charged with telling fortunes contrary to the village ordinances and were fined $5 and costs each and also ordered to get out of town.

*Copper Country Evening News*, September 18, 1909

A band of gypsies, comprising three women, two men and eleven children, of all ages, from an infant in arms up to 15 years of age, paid a visit to the South Shore depot this morning. They came in on this morning's South Shore train from Duluth and are now housed in the baggage department at the depot. The two men are out scouting around for a place to pitch their tents. Their effort will be vain as far as Red Jacket is concerned. Chief Trudell states that no gypsies will be allowed to locate in the village.

Hundreds of people visited the depot this morning to get a look at the dark-eyed, swarthy-skinned natives of southern Europe. One of the women, in particular, is a brunette of a striking appearance. The women and children do not talk English. All of the children, with the exception of the two oldest, are thinly clad. All appear healthy, however, and are apparently well fed.[6]

## Southwestern Michigan

> Celebrations are the glue that binds Roma to their families and communi-
> ties. Both in the Balkans and in the diaspora, community members not only
> gather regularly for events, most of which include music and dance, but
> also plan them well ahead of time and discuss them long afterward; events
> thus have a long symbolic life.[7]

Romanies traveled back and forth between Chicago, Illinois, and Benton
Harbor, Michigan. Perhaps one of the earliest nondiscriminatory portraits
of Romanies is Irving Brown's *Gypsy Fires in America* (1922). Fascinated by
the Romanies, Brown traveled in the early twentieth century throughout the
United States and Europe to discover and familiarize himself with them. He
describes a wedding he attended at "a weird spot on the edge of the dunes,
at the lower end of Lake Michigan, some miles across the state line from Illinois"[8]—presumably in Indiana. While it is not literally Michigan, for anyone
who has traveled between Illinois and Michigan, the description of the scene
feels close enough—on the sand dunes along Lake Michigan.

Brown spoke some Romani. He wrote, "I answered them, casually letting
fall the information that I was part Romani. It had not been hard to convince
myself of this; but all the non-Gypsies to whom I have told it have simply
been amused. As for brazenly telling it to a Gypsy, it was so presumptu-
ous—that it was believed."[9] While some scholars are critical of his method
of learning about the Romanies, nevertheless he wrote beautiful, poetic
prose descriptions and observations of their lives nearly one hundred years
ago, giving us a taste for their lifestyle—much like a travel log, journal, or
documentary film.

The bridal couple, which had traveled through much of Europe and North
and South America, was then living in Chicago in the early 1920s. Two different groups of Romanies were present at the wedding—those who had
left Europe and immigrated via Latin America to the United States, settling
in Chicago, and those whose musician families originally had come from
Hungary and Slovakia and had also settled in Chicago. Brown exquisitely
captures the wedding event, which ultimately had many twists and turns.
He allows us to not only visualize but also hear the music of the stringed
instruments, including the traditional cimbalom, vocalists, the sound of

the wind, and the voice of water lapping on Lake Michigan shores. During the duration of the three-day wedding events, the Romanies feasted on pig, sheep, and turkey, which they roasted on spits over coals, as well as chicken soups, breads, and cakes.

> On the opposite side of the fire an orchestra of Hungarian gypsies was play-ing with dash and abandon. At the last minute someone had discovered them in a saloon in South Chicago, playing to the "Hunkies" from the steel mills, and had engaged them in place of a Polish band that had previously been hired. The first violin, the leader, was from the Banat, and played a great number of Slavic, Magyar, and Rumanian songs and dances, as well as many that were purely Romani. The cembalist [sic], the second violin, and the bass viol played the accompaniments though by instinct, following the leader through a maze of unfamiliar melodies. . . .
>
> The scene was barbaric. The black hair of the Romanies melted into the blackness of the night. The firelight gleamed in flashing eyes. It shone on the red coral, the large yellow beads, and the necklaces of golden coins of the women. Their red and orange dresses turned and twisted like the tongues of flame. Two little tots had taken their mothers' crimson *diklos* and were dancing voluptuously, prolonging the undulations of their supple bodies with the snake-like movements of the kerchiefs.[10]

Shannon McRae posted some memories on the Benton Harbor and St. Joseph Facebook page.

> A long time ago (a couple of years probably, but eons in Internet history), somebody here posted a mention of a gypsy encampment along the St Joe River. I just tracked down what was going on. A Queen of the Gypsies, Anna Mitchell, lived here, and died on August 31st, 1953. There was a three-week vigil, with apparently dozens of families mostly camping out at the funeral home and many other open spaces. Apparently, the community was fairly nice to them, even though the newspaper story freaks out about how many, many Gypsies there were, and how dramatic the funeral (apparently two of her sons, pall-bearers, passed out from the heat by the bier at Florin chapel shortly before the funeral). Interestingly enough, her funeral Mass

was said at St. John's Catholic. The funeral procession included 27 carloads of Gypsies, plus funeral home, police and fire department cars. . . . Police estimated each car had 8 to 10 passengers. 150 local residents were also in attendance at the Church. This is from the *News Palladium*, stories between August 1st and September 2, 1953.[11]

Contrary to most other twentieth-century newspaper articles, the stories in the *News Palladium* of Benton Harbor are surprisingly quite favorable about the Romanies attending a vigil. The Romanies were grateful to the Benton Harbor community of local residents, hospital staff, and police department. The journalist paints a portrait of the Romanies camped there while keeping a vigil for their dying Gypsy Queen Annie Mitchell and the local people of Benton Harbor.[12] Because of the three-week vigil, the journalist had an opportunity and challenge to document the events from many perspectives and interviewed different people in great detail about both the visitors' and the local residents' interactions. These news stories provide a rare window of opportunity to observe the events without editorializing. A local farmer even let the Romanies camp on his property. The Romanies were grateful and invited all the townspeople to the funeral. The reporter spoke to Annie Mitchell's husband and sons.

This is an excerpt from one of the many articles that appeared in the *News Palladium* in Benton Harbor over the three-week period.

"Gypsies Are Grateful for City's Kindness, Public Invited to Queen's Funeral," *News Palladium*, Benton Harbor, Michigan, September 1, 1953

Standing a month-long vigil at the bedside of their dying queen, a tribe of gypsies have found friends and kindness in Benton Harbor.

That's what they told a *News Palladium* reporter last night as they gathered at the Florin Funeral Home here around the candlelighted [*sic*] bier of their matriarch, Mrs. Annie Mitchell. "Put in your paper that we invited everyone to come and see our mother, and that we welcome the public to the funeral," said several of Mrs. Mitchell's seven living sons.[13]

And her husband, William Mitchell, a grizzled veteran of nomadic travels across a continent, explained,

"Your newspaper has said nice things about us. The people here in Benton Harbor have been good. They treat us just like anyone else. And they grieve with us because our head woman dies."

A son added: "No one here gives us trouble. Your hospital has been so kind to us; the police department is very good—They give us the protection we need while we are here."[14]

## Angeline Rosemarie M.'s Story

Angeline Rosemarie M., a young woman who lives in Michigan, shared her story about her family who had migrated to southwestern Michigan. She is a composite of multiethnic groups who came to America from Europe and eventually moved to Michigan. Angeline Rosemarie M.'s relatives included musicians, vaudeville performers, and a scientist. Some of her relatives on her grandfather's side were Romanies from Galicia in Europe who were part of a band. She said that her great-grandmother Clara's family's Royal Hungarian Gypsy Band performed in Europe—in Hungary, Russia, the Ukraine and elsewhere. They fled Europe to escape persecution in the late nineteenth century and went to Chicago. Angeline Rosemarie M. said that the band played at the World's Columbian Exposition in 1893, which was also called the Chicago World's Fair and sometimes known as the "the fair that changed the world." Their descendants eventually came to Benton Harbor/St. Joseph, Michigan.

As a child, Angeline Rosemarie M. was very close with her great-grandmother Clara, who was the matriarch of the family and shared family stories with her. She has fond memories of spending time with Clara in St. Joseph/Benton Harbor. Clara died in her nineties in 1990.

Other family members were Irish Gypsy Travellers who were a vaudeville troupe. She thinks they left Ireland because of persecution and went to New York and then Chicago. Their descendants eventually came to Michigan. Angeline Rosemarie M. was also very close with her grandmother, Rosemarie, for whom she is named, and is very proud that her grandma read tea leaves and palms for her classmates in kindergarten or first grade.

Angeline Rosemarie M. said, "My relatives and I never lost our heritage inside our skins or our identity even if we were forced to walk away from our heritage in the outside world."

These brief snippets of stories provide a glimpse into the presence of Romanies throughout Michigan, primarily in the twentieth century. The next stories tell us about the Hungarian-Slovak Romanies who immigrated to the Midwest from Europe and then migrated to Michigan following the Hungarian immigrants to play their music in Hungarian restaurants and bars.

# Hungarian-Slovak Romani Music in Delray

The music never left or never leaves us, you know? It runs in our veins. If a Gypsy hears a beautiful song, it hits us like, "Oh my goodness," and the heart keeps feeling it very deeply. That will never, ever go away. It's just something that's in your blood. I don't know how to best describe it. Music is at the top of our list of what defines us.

—Chris Slepsky, Romani multi-instrumentalist

Hungarian-Slovak Romani families, many of them descendants of famous Romani musicians, began to immigrate to the United States from Europe in the 1880s. Originally, they came from the village of Kassa, Hungary (now Kosice, Slovakia) and other communities, and followed the Hungarians who had settled in Cleveland and Youngstown, Ohio, and in Braddock, Pennsylvania. Along with other immigrants, they worked in the steel mills, as well as in stores, pharmacies, groceries, restaurants, taverns, and the entertainment industry.[1]

The Romanies then followed the Hungarians to Michigan.

They were attracted by the job opportunities in factories, foundries, and manufacturing plants during a particularly brisk industrial boom in the region. . . . Originally from small and economically disadvantaged rural villages in Hungary, they first tried their luck with farm work in the United States and Canada or worked in mines in West Virginia, Kentucky, Pennsylvania, and the Upper Peninsula of Michigan. Some of them left factory jobs in Ohio, Illinois, and Indiana.[2]

More specific information is known about the Hungarian-Slovak Romanies who migrated primarily from Braddock, Pennsylvania, to Delray than those other Romanies who traveled around and through Michigan over many years, often in caravans. "The group commonly referred to in the United States as Hungarian Gypsies represents only one of Hungary's four major Gypsy groups. Most Hungarian Gypsies emigrated [sic] to North America from northern Hungary (now Slovakia) during the first two decades of this century."[3] These were "the Bashaldey or 'Hungarian-Slovak Roma.' They are by far outnumbered in Michigan by the Vlax Roma and Romanichal Roma."[4]

The Hungarian immigrants worked for Henry Ford for five dollars a day—more than they had earned in the steel mills in the Pittsburgh area— and opened up restaurants and bars where the Romanies then played their music. Anthropologist Éva V. Darvas-Huseby wrote,

> Delray . . . was a magnet for Windsorites (from Canada), who crossed over to Detroit by bridge, ferry-boat and tunnel, to visit relatives, to attend churches or church-functions, to dine and dance at favorite hot-spots (Ne Tovabb, Kovacs Bar, Hungarian Village and so many others) to the beat of Gypsy orchestras (Janos Brenkacs, Ziggy Bela), to buy imported foods from Hungary (preserves, paprika from Szeged, salamis, etc.) and of course to attend the movie theatre which featured Hungarian film stars such as Javor Pal, Kabos Gyula.[5]

Sometimes they also performed music in Windsor, and in turn, those Romanies who lived in Windsor sometimes came to perform in Delray.[6] Over the years, the Hungarian-Slovak Romanies along with other immigrants moved out of Delray, particularly to the Dearborn area, including Allen Park, Southgate, and Warren, and even to Nevada, performing in a variety of venues in hotels, nightclubs, and bars. As the community has aged, most of the younger generations have been moving away from music careers. Today, they all still travel back and forth to Braddock, Cleveland, and Chicago to visit, attend family and friends' celebrations, and perform in music gigs.

## Early Delray

According to sociologist Marlene Sway, research about the Romanies in the United States first appeared in publications in 1975, except for one important article back in 1936 by sociologist Erdmann Doane Beynon, who studied Hungarian immigrants in Detroit and then the Romani immigrants. "Viewing the Gypsy community as an appendage of the Hungarian community, Beynon observed that most of the Gypsies were musicians who earned a living by playing at religious and secular festivities held in the newborn Hungarian-American community."[7] Beynon's rare, historical documentation of Romanies in the United States portrays the growing, vibrant community in Delray. He wrote,

> The avowed purpose of the Hungarian Gypsies in their migration to Detroit was . . . to furnish music for the various entertainments, which constitute the major part of the leisure-time activities of a Hungarian group. . . . This situation led to an increased migration of musician Gypsies to Detroit, to a raising of the fee for their services, and to an effort by Gypsies who were not already professional musicians to share in this lucrative employment.[8]

Gene Scott of the Detroit Retired City Employees Association was fascinated by the depth and wealth of Detroit's history and produced a book as a Detroit 300 Partners Program. He shed light on the challenges of coping with Detroit's environmental pollution, specifically in Delray.

> From the beginning, the people of Delray struggled daily to survive in the midst of heavy manufacturing, everything from copper pots to trains, in the factories along West Jefferson (then called River Road). A large section of the village was developed for the International Exposition Grounds—a favorite amusement center for Detroiters in the 1890s and in 1894, the Michigan State Fair. But the fun didn't last long, not with pervasive factory fumes in the air. A soda-ash processing plant went up on the old fairgrounds. . . .

During the Great Depression people came from all over to hear the Gypsy music on the streets of Delray, but by the 1940s, most of the older groups were moving away.[9]

The industrial companies included the Fisher Glue Plant and the Solvay Chemical Company, Great Lakes Steel, Detroit Edison, Fleetwood Body, Allied Chemicals, and Peerless Cement.[10]

### Romani Musicians Perform in a Variety of Venues

During the twentieth century, the Hungarian-Slovak Romani community of Delray supported a rich musical scene. While musicians originally played traditional Romani and Hungarian music, they adapted and accommodated to the changing demands, requests, and opportunities from the larger society and expanded their repertoire and venues. They showed amazing versatility and innovation over time as they learned all kinds of music for a variety of audiences. In addition to playing at festivals, weddings, funerals, and picnics, they played "old-time dance music" for Henry Ford's events and his radio shows, as well as for the Hungarian Radio Hour, in restaurants and bars (many of them Hungarian), on records, and in concerts for the Federal Music Project as part of the Works Progress Administration (WPA, renamed the Works Projects Administration in 1939). As anthropologist Carol Silverman says, "Music is the vehicle for enacting social relationships and enhancing status. It is also a commodity to sell to non-Roma and other Roma."[11]

While the Romanies performed for the non-Romani or *gadjé* communities, they also gathered together to play music for their own family, social and cultural events, and rites of passage. Steve Piskor, who introduced me to the Hungarian-Slovak Romanies (or as he prefers to say, Gypsies) of Delray, talks about the importance of music in a Romani's life in his book.

> He or she starts learning an instrument at an early age, between five and ten years old. The instruments are handed down. Most of the Gypsies wanted their sons to play violin and become a *primas* (lead violinist).[12]

While the Romani have traditionally played the violin, they also play a variety of other instruments, including keyboard instruments, guitar, saxophone, and cimbalom. The cimbalom is an elaborate stringed instrument of the dulcimer family used in small ensembles by Central European Romani. It has a trapezoidal body that stands on four legs. It has a chromatic range of four octaves and, unlike other dulcimers, a pedal mechanism for damping the strings. The cimbalom has about 125 metal strings, with 3 to 5 strings per note. Some of the strings have two or three bridges along their length. The musician, who plays in a seated position, strikes the strings with two small, spoon-shaped wooden hammers, one held in each hand. The hammers are covered with either hard or soft leather, depending on the tone quality desired.[13] "Cimbaloms were brought over in immigrant ships, imported from Hungarian manufacturers, and built in America by immigrants and their children."[14]

## Romani Musicians Play with Henry Ford

Henry Ford had an affinity for dance music and Romani musicians. In 1924, he created the "Henry Ford Old Fashioned Dance Orchestra" to try to preserve old-fashioned music and counteract the new wave of jazz.

> Ford loved the violin, and when he was alone in his office, he often played one of the violins from his collection, including his $75,000, 1703 Stradivarius. . . . He often sponsored fiddle and square dance competitions . . . to get the young ones back into the old-time music and dancing. . . .
>
> The orchestra consisted of a violin, a sousaphone (tuba) or bass fiddle, a dulcimer, and a cimbalom. . . . The cimbalom player was a Gypsy from Braddock by the name of William Hallup; the Gypsies called him "Skinny." Hallup was one of the first Roma to move to Detroit from Braddock Pennsylvania.[15]

Eugene J. Farkas, an immigrant from Kald, Hungary, became an engineer for the Ford Motor Company. Ford asked him to find a cimbalom player for his music band, which he did. During an oral history interview conducted in 1954, Farkas reminisced,

> They started to play some Hungarian pieces, which was all right. It was all nice music, but it didn't impress Mr. Ford very much I noticed. So, I said,

*Figure 5. Henry Ford Playing with His Old-Time Dance Orchestra of Musicians, 1933.*
From left to right: *Henry Ford, William Hallup, Maurice Castel, Clayton Perry, and Edwin Baxter. Image from the Collections of The Henry Ford.*

if Mr. Ford had any particular pieces that he would like to hear, these boys could play anything. He had some sheet music of different things that probably these fellows never heard of before. I remember one very well, "When you and I were young, Maggie." Right away they started to play that, and they played it beautifully. I could see the expression on Mr. Ford's face was entirely different. . . .

The Romani musicians worried that they could injure themselves working in the factory and then they would not be able to play their music. Initially some of them worked in the plant, but eventually they no longer had to. Mr. Ford suggested that we take the whole band and put them to work in the factory. Well, they weren't very enthused. . . . "Well, we can't work on machines. Suppose our hands got hurt. We'll never be able to play again." They were perfectly right.[16]

Henry Ford was also keen on using radio for multiple purposes.

The first broadcasting station to feature entertainment came on the air in 1920: KDKA was the Western Electric & Manufacturing Company of East Pittsburgh. The first in Michigan was 8MK (WWJ), the *Detroit News*, August 20, 1920. Ford Motor Company needed better equipment and a "broadcast" license to address the public likewise. Henry Ford favored such a move because he not only was anxious to control the expression of his ideas on many issues but also wanted to broadcast old-time music and possibly advertise Ford cars. . . .

The early Ford public broadcasts used talent largely from the ranks of Ford employees. The Ford Motor Company Highland Park Orchestra, the River Rouge Orchestra, and the Ford Hungarian Gypsy Orchestra were used extensively.[17]

## Hungarian Radio Hour

Radio programs provided yet another opportunity for Romani musicians to perform. "At this time the Hungarian ethnic radio and press began to flourish, as did amateur plays, poetry and prose readings, church and cultural center suppers, dances, and such. . . . Starting an ethnic radio program was a very important process for the Hungarian American community in the period between the two World Wars and beyond."[18]

Erno Pálos, a Jewish immigrant from Hungary, originally went to Cleveland and then migrated to Michigan in the early 1930s.

> Mr. Pálos was already the publisher of the local weekly paper, the *Detroiti Magyarság*—Detroit Hungarians—when on 19 January 1936 he started a new venture, a radio program, the Hungarian Rhapsody Hour. . . . Mr. Pálos broadcast live music and skits, performed by amateur actors and actresses, musicians and vocalists, Gypsy orchestras, and chamber music groups, as well as children's recitals.[19]

## Romanies Perform in Hungarian Restaurants and Bars and on the Streets

The Hungarian Slovakian Romanies performed their music in Hungarian restaurants and bars and on the streets of Delray as early as 1907.

*Figure 6. Hungarian Village Restaurant, 1930s. Photo courtesy of Burton Collection, Detroit Public Library.*

In the 1930s the Hungarian population of Detroit was growing as well as the Gypsy population. Hungarian restaurants and clubs were opening, such as the Hungarian Village Restaurant. Gypsy music was in demand. . . . Many of the young Gypsy musicians from Braddock [Pennsylvania] were now adult Gypsies in Detroit. This new era of Gypsies in Detroit would go on to produce some of the finest Gypsy musicians.[20]

The original Hungarian Village Restaurant has since been razed. A second restaurant, which had opened in nearby Springwell, was sold.

Robert Takacs, whose parents emigrated from Hungary, shared warm memories of growing up in Delray. He also enjoyed listening to the Romani perform music in Delray at weddings, picnics, and dances, and at Estral Beach on Lake Erie in the summer months.

I'll tell you, growing up in Delray—it was a good life. The people working all the time. They kept the area very neat. The streets were nice and clean.

People kept their grasses cut nice and everything, and you would see them outside, sitting on the sidewalk on the nice warm days. . . . There were no problems, no crime, nothing. You didn't have to worry about walking the streets at dark, leaving your home open. You could go to church and you could leave your stuff on the stove being cooked, and nobody would ever enter your home or nothing like that. People were always friendly with one another. . . . The women worked together doing different things. The kids—we'd go out and play in the field. . . . We'd build our own skating ponds in the winter.

## Kovacs Bar in Delray

Kovacs Bar was a regular venue for Romani musicians. A neighborhood bar and restaurant, it was established around 1944 by Hungarians who had migrated from Ohio to Delray. Located on the north side of West Jefferson Avenue, the building was built around 1889. Most customers worked in the local factories and frequented the bar for socializing and good food.[21]

Residents spoke Hungarian in Lehostksy's Bakery, Zolkower's Department Store, the Delray Meat Market, and Rozi Neni's Bar. They danced at the Verhovay and the Petofi social clubs, ate chicken paprikash at Al's Lounge and walnut torte at the fancy Pastry Shop, and bought hurka (rice sausage) at Szabo's Meat Market (closed in 1995). . . . Many of the patrons were employed at Solvay Process, Peninsular Stove, International Salt Mine, Revere Copper & Brass, and the Ford Rouge Plant.[22]

One longtime patron of Kovacs, Eddie Kaysackar, a freight driver for Yellow Transportation, talked about his memories of Kovacs—in particular about seeing Danny Devito, who used to come into Kovacs when filmmakers were shooting the movie *Hoffa* back in the 1970s.[23] Kovacs Bar was demolished on November 6, 2017, to make way for the construction of the Gordy Howe Bridge.[24]

## Who Were the Hungarian-Slovak Romani Musicians?

Many multitalented, multigenerational family Romani musicians have a rich
history in Michigan and elsewhere.

### Violinist Ziggy Bela's Story (Julius Margitza)

Ziggy Bela (name and spellings vary), whose real name was Julius Margitza,
was the most famous violinist from the Delray community who performed
traditional Romani music. As a child, Ziggy moved from Braddock, Pennsylvania, to Delray, where he played at many establishments, including Kovacs
and the Hungarian Village Restaurant. Many family members also became
well-known, talented musicians.

In an article, "The Open Road: It's Lost Its Old Attraction for Many of
Detroit's Gypsies," in the *Detroit Free Press* (April 8, 1951), staff writer James
S. Pooler interviewed Ziggy Bella.

> "Of course, I cannot speak of the Russian or other tribes," said Ziggy Bella.
> "They are mostly traders and fortune tellers and the open road still calls to
> them. The first warm wind and they probably are on their roving again. But
> me . . . I love the city."
>
> Bella, of 78894 Medina, has shot down some roots here. For 12 years he
> has been a violinist at the Hungarian Village . . . which is a remarkably long
> time for a gypsy to stay any place.
>
> Ziggy wanted Detroit to understand there are differences in gypsies.
> "I am a Hungarian gypsy," he said. "We are musicians. So are the Roma-
> nian gypsies. We do not monkey around with trying to tell you what will
> happen to you tomorrow. We want to make you happy or sad with our
> music today."
>
> And there are plenty of Hungarian gypsies in Detroit doing that. Ziggy
> guessed there were 200 Hungarian gypsies in Detroit—And about 60 of
> them musicians.
>
> "They work days in the automobile plants. Nights and weekends, they
> make music," he said.
>
> He said there were a lot of gypsy orchestras in Detroit—Four or five-man
> combinations who play the "strings" usually in combination of two violins,
> a cimbalom, viola and bass.
>
> He said . . . "We thought a little sadly . . . that some of the younger gypsy

*Figure 7. Ziggy Bella playing his violin at his son Julius's funeral. Photo by Michael S. Green. Reprinted courtesy of the* Detroit News.

musicians, they get together and hold a jam session. Of course, it still has an overtone of Hungarian music which is something."

They love music so well they have no king. The best fiddler in any community usually is top man. Ziggy was too modest to say so but—Well, if the gypsy king wore a crown it probably would rest on his head."[25]

Piskor said that over the years Romanies from communities throughout the United States came together to grieve at family and friends' funerals. "Typically, a funeral would last three to four days, and there was always a lot of music, food, and drink. On the morning of the funeral, musicians would gather to play . . . sometimes as many as fifty to seventy-five. . . . The music was sad and slow, in the fashion of the *halgato*, a Hungarian term for slow Gypsy music."[26]

In the 1950s, Ziggy Bela started his famous "Gypsy Picnic" Concerts.

Within a few years, the concerts were attracting national attention and hundreds of people were attending the event to see as many as fifty to sixty

Gypsy musicians led by Ziggy Bela, under the musical direction of Gus
Horvath. . . . The Gypsy Picnics went on for over twenty years and became
one of Detroit's best-known events."[27]

According to the back cover of a record "Dreams of Budapest, Bela Ziggy and
His Famous Gypsy Orchestra," produced by the B and F Record Company
in Cleveland Ohio,

> Bela Ziggy is most qualified to express the pleasing artistry of Gypsy music
> with such warmth and devotion. He and his singing violin heading a sup-
> porting orchestra recruited from the best musicians, is now heard for the
> first time on LP records. His truly fine rendition of tunes is so ably molded
> into folk songs, waltzes, tangos, rhumbas, etc.
>
> Coming from a musical family, his entire family background is con-
> nected with music, his Aunt Countess Verona was the greatest cimbalom
> player in the world. . . . Rising in a spectacularly short time in his profession,
> he has been Musical Director of the biggest hotel chains and was specifi-
> cally chosen to play private concerts for the great names in the Art of Music
> Festival held in Detroit, Michigan. . . . [28]

Perhaps the most original, innovative jazz musician was the French Romani Django Reinhardt—"one man, one guitar, two fingers, six strings, an
infinity of notes."[29] In 1946, he came to the United States to "tour as a special
guest soloist with Duke Ellington's Orchestra, he spread his jazz not only to
the jazz faithful but also to a hidden audience."[30]

He went to the Hungarian Village Restaurant in 1946 where he heard
Ziggy Bela play.

> After playing the tour finale in Detroit on the night of December 7, 1946,
> Django and his band mates from Duke's orchestra were directed across
> town to Dearborn's Hungarian Village, [sic, Delray] a swank nightspot that
> was the height of Detroit fashion. While they dined, they were serenaded by
> Romani Violinist Ziggy Bella. . . . Yet it was Ziggy's son, ten-year old violinist
> Julius Margitza, who was most thrilled by the French Gypsy's visit. Julius
> was also playing that night at the Hungarian Village, and according to fam-
> ily legend, Django joined in. Hearing Django, Julius was moved to tune his

violin to jazz. Eighteen years later in 1964, Julius—playing under the name
Julio Bella—would release the first album of American Gypsy jazz, *The Hot
Jazz Violin of Julio Bella and His Quartette*.[31] Julio died in Dearborn on April
16, 1988. He was only fifty-four.[32]

In 1989, Ziggy performed at the Festival of Michigan Folk Life in East Lansing. He suffered a heart attack two days later and died.

A dozen violinists led a block-long procession to Holy Cross Roman
Catholic Church. "His brother Alex Bella led the violinists, three bass players
and three guitarists in a final tribute to the musician."[33]

Musical talent and abilities often run multigenerationally throughout
many members of Romani families. Several relatives of Ziggy Bela shared
their stories. Ziggy's nephew, Richard Margitza, played in the Detroit Symphony Orchestra for almost forty years and retired to the Las Vegas area.
Richard's father, Louis, who was Ziggy Bela's brother, was a violinist and
owner of a violin repair shop, the Budapest String Shop, in Detroit.

Richard Margitza said,

> I studied with Mischa Mischakoff who was the concertmaster with Toscanini and the NBC Symphony Orchestra. He was the concertmaster of the
> Detroit Symphony Orchestra at the time. . . . Then, I auditioned with the
> Detroit Symphony Orchestra. . . . I made the audition, they hired me, and I
> was with the orchestra for thirty-seven years. I played all over the world in
> all the great symphony orchestra halls. . . . Then, I also played with the Motown Record Corporation. You know, Michael Jackson and the Supremes.

Richard Margitza's son, Rick, a well-known, international saxophonist,
performer, composer, and music professor, now lives in Paris. His dad and
his mom, Eleanor Margitza, are so very proud of him. Eleanor Margitza said,
"Rick studied and thank God, he was given a gift. Because he's a writer, an
arranger, teacher, you name it, he does it in jazz music."

Rick Margitza studied classical saxophone with Donald Sinta at the
University of Michigan, and jazz with Sonny Stitt, Gerry Niewood, Michael
Brecker, and David Liebman. He studied at Wayne State University, the Berklee School of Music in Boston, and the University of Miami, and graduated
with a bachelor's degree in music from Loyola University in New Orleans.

*Figure 8. Rick Margitza.*
*Photo courtesy Ursula K.*

He has performed and/or recorded with many famous musicians, including McCoy Tyner, Bobby Hutcherson, Tony Williams, Eddie Gomez, Chick Corea, Maria Schneider, Dave Douglas, and Miles Davis. He has led his own band and performed in clubs, concert halls, and festivals worldwide. Rick's most recent recording, *Bohemia*, on the French label Nocturne, is his most personal to date, in which he explores his Gypsy roots by tracing Romanies' origin from India across Eastern Europe.

Rick Margitza said,

> There are definitely some misunderstood aspects with the Gypsies, especially . . . in Romania. Anti-Gypsy sentiments that still are in Germany and Austria. It's pretty sad to see that. But, in general it's not as misunderstood as it is in the States. And I think that's just because there hasn't been that much correct information or just information in general about where the Gypsies really are and where they came from.

I think it's just the true definition of ignorance, which means unin-
formed; maybe they're not as curious and it could be the same reason as
why jazz and the arts are not as respected here. It's just an older culture in
Europe in general. There's been maybe longer time for people to understand what's going on. And also, in Europe, people are not ashamed to say
they're Gypsies. I think here for a long time, in our culture we were told just
say you're Hungarian, don't say you're Gypsy, because when you say that,
people immediately assume that you steal, and you tell fortunes and stuff
that you see in movies.

### Cimbalist Gus Horvath's Story

Another well-known Hungarian Romani American musician, Gus Horvath,
a colleague of Ziggy Bela, was born in Braddock, Pennsylvania, in 1916 and
moved to Delray, where he lived for many years. He was one of the last
Romani to leave Delray to move to Dearborn Heights. "He began studying
cimbalom with Louis (Bum) Ballog; he furthered his studies in New York
with the great cimbalom player Zsiga Bela. Horvath's cimbalom skills were
among the best, and he was known throughout America, Canada, and Europe. Gus made many recordings and performed in many of the finest places.

*Figure 9. Gus Horvath's cimbalom from Michigan State University Museum. Note all
the elaborate decorations he used to embellish his instrument.*

In 1948 he purchased a Hungarian cimbalom and flamboyantly embellished it himself . . . Horvath died in 2001."[34]

The Gus Horvath Collection at Michigan State University includes his last cimbalom, copies of his photo albums and scrapbooks, sheet music, hammers, bills of sale for musical instruments, tools and equipment Gus used to embellish his instruments, handbills, and newspaper clippings. These materials highlight Gus Horvath's long musical career and provide context to augment our understanding of Gus, his instruments, and the community of musicians.

Family and friends shared their memories about Gus Horvath. His daughter, Elaine Horvath Moise, said,

> We'd go out at night. We'd get all dressed up and go out. We'd walk down the street, and everybody would call out. It was just enjoyable, living there. This is what we heard all the time, was Gypsy music. . . . You never were alone, there was always somebody coming or going, and we would just enjoy all of them. We always had musicians. My father loved music, so he always had the older men musicians coming over my house. They would have drinks, play the music and enjoy that. And that's what they loved to do, that was their thing, to play their instruments. Mostly Gypsy. Hungarian-Gypsy music. . . . He was a perfectionist.

Victor Moise, son of Elaine Horvath Moise and grandson of Gus Horvath, said his parents made his brothers and him take piano lessons as children. "My grandfather . . . would come in the back room where we were practicing. . . . And he would go like 'Oh God, they ruined my life. My grandsons are 'throgeds.' That's the worst insult you can call a Gypsy, meaning lacking musical talent. All five of us wanted to play hockey. We wanted to be carrying on the legacy of my father. We weren't concerned with Gypsy music when we were younger. . . . Well, my brothers and I appreciate it now, the musical heritage."

Angelina Moise Malavenda, Gus Horvath's great-granddaughter, said,

> My grandfather was a man with a few words, like an outsider looking in; he would come off a little intimidating, but he had a soft side for his

great-grandchildren. He loved us, and spoiled my dad, he was the first born, the first grandchild. His cimbalom, which is his musical instrument he played, that was his baby. I just remember him taking care of that at all times and remaking his. My father instilled in all of my cousins and me that it is very important to continue learning, educating ourselves on an unfortunately dying breed in America, of 100 percent purebred Gypsies; from the love of music and to the overall culture that we still appreciate and understand it passing our knowledge and memories down generation to generation.

Friends of Gus Horvath also shared their memories of Gus. Musician William Tyler White, who owns the White Bros. Music in Bath, Michigan, used to listen to the Romanies play in Delray back in the 1970s and hung out with them after they played. He even played with Gus Horvath years ago at Greenfield Village and actually owns one of Gus Horvath's basses.

My favorite memories are just watching him play or listening to him play. He was always a funny guy to talk to, always had a good word. He was always a promoter, which is why he decorated the base on the cimbalom, 'cause that would make it look fancy. We gotta look fancy! I'm the promoter!

Alex Sagady Jr. is an environmental consultant in East Lansing. His father was a senior project engineer at General Motors, whose parents had immigrated to the Delray area from Hungary.

I don't know exactly when my father and Gus Horvath met and began playing music together. I can remember Horvath and my father when I was five years old so that would be at least 1955, but I believe they probably met sometime in the 1940s.

When my father and Gus Horvath played a gig together, my father would end up hauling both his "made from scratch" cimbalom so it could be seen being played by Horvath along with his string bass which he was able to fit both in the big Chevy station wagon my father owned. . . . I remember my father bringing me to Gus Horvath's home a couple of times. . . .

In September 1972, Gus Horvath was with my father the day he died at age 57 of a coronary heart attack. My father, Gus Horvath, and some other Roma musicians were playing for a reception at Cobo Hall. . . . Horvath organized a group of musicians who played Hungarian music at my father's funeral at the Ford Funeral Home in Centerline Michigan where I grew up.

## Guitarist and Vocalist Billy Rose's Story

Well-known guitarist and vocalist Billy Rose reminisced about his musical career. Through the years he has played both traditional Gypsy music and jazz standards and has performed in Delray, Downtown Detroit, and throughout the Midwest. Today, he plays in the Metro Detroit area with his son, Chris Slepsky, and his granddaughter Lauren Slepsky-Chicko, and still plays Gypsy concerts with a small, traditional ensemble throughout the Midwest.

It was about 1947. I was playing in Downtown Detroit in a beautiful Italian restaurant called Giovanni's on Temple and Woodward Avenue. I was only about 17 years old. We used to play there from two until five o'clock in the morning, when all the other bars and restaurants would close. I met a lot of great entertainers that would come in there.

That's me with Bob Hope when I was 17 years old. We played for him at Giovanni's. He and his singer, Billy Farrell, would come in all the time. Many great entertainers and movie stars would come there as well, including Anthony Quinn. They would finish their own performances and would come to Giovanni's around two o'clock in the morning for late-night dining and entertainment.

Bob Hope told me, "You've gotta sing my songs." He made a popular song that was a big hit, called "Circus." It was sung and made popular by Billy Farrell. I later recorded this song on my album *We Live in a World*. (*sings*) "Circus, life at the circus, it's a hectic thing, the moon was a toy balloon . . ." I also recorded a few other songs at the studio, by the request of Anthony Quinn.

Our life revolves around family, food, and music. I especially love our traditional Gypsy music. Our Gypsy music used to thrive, as we would play in large ensembles and orchestras, extending back many centuries. For many years, I used to perform with many large ensembles. Unfortunately, our traditional Gypsy music is dying out as the music of our time has

*Figure 10. Billy Rose* (left), *at age 17, performs for Bob Hope at Giovanni's Restaurant in Detroit, which has since closed. Photo courtesy Billy Rose.*

changed. I still play with a small Gypsy ensemble on Sundays and perform several concerts in the Midwest throughout the year.

Our Gypsy music has been passed down for generations. My father, Arpad Slepsky, was also a musician. He played the viola and performed the role of a second violinist. His father, John Slepsky, was also a musician who would perform in New York and Slovakia. My maternal grandfather, Louis Rakoczi, was a violinist and orchestra leader who performed with a large Gypsy orchestra in Braddock, Pennsylvania, where most of our Roma community settled in America once they immigrated from Europe in the 1890s. Our culture and music really thrived in Braddock, Pennsylvania, where I was born, and also in Delray, where our community settled once we migrated to the Detroit area in the 1930s and 1940s.

Lauren Slepsky-Chicko, Billy Rose's granddaughter, inherited her talent and love and desire to perform vocal music not only from the paternal side of her family but also from her maternal grandmother, Evelyn Horvath Hallup. Her grandmother's love of music was passed down from her own father, William Hallup, who had played with Henry Ford in his dance orchestra. Evelyn Hallup said,

> All I ever wanted to do, all of my life, was to sing and listen to beautiful music. It's just something that's inside you. You don't know how, why, or when, it's just something that's within you. You know that all you want to do is sing and deeply feel the music.

### Keyboard Player Don De Andre's Story

Multitalented keyboard musician Don De Andre had an eclectic musical career. He was born in Uniontown, Pennsylvania, and lived in many places, including Cleveland and Chicago. He played in Delray and at hotels, bars, and restaurants throughout the country and performed "backup" for many celebrities and in different parts of the country. He performed with comedians Joey Bishop and Phil Tucker. He played at famous nightclubs including Chez Paree in Chicago, and on the ferry from Detroit to Boblo Island.

Don De Andre said that when his name was on the marquee, "That was one of the biggest things in my life! Vegas, headline! Vegas is what's considered the finest place you wanna do. Headline a club or casino one year." In Dearborn, he worked with John Trudell at the Hyatt Regency. He also worked with Billy Eckstine, Peggy Lee, Leslie Uggams, and Tina Turner. Now in retirement in Las Vegas, Don De Andre has taught his grandson to play and backs up for one of his granddaughters.

De Andre's daughter, Renee Andrea Bandy, a vocalist, was born in Chicago, moved to Delray where she grew up, and now lives in Las Vegas. She raised her own family and now takes care of her father.

*Figure 11. In 1980 in Detroit, Don De Andre* (right) *played with Billy Eckstine, who was a popular singer, songwriter, and trumpet player, known for his bebop music. Photo courtesy Don De Andre.*

My mom would tell me as a little girl, "Don't you go out of the yard. The Gypsies will steal you. Don't go out in the yard, those Gypsies are gonna steal you." So I wouldn't go out of the yard, because, I feared the Gypsies and I was a Gypsy. But we are different. Like I said, there's more education involved. We have some Roma that are eye doctors. We have some Roma that are very well-known musicians, that worked with Miles Davis and, and, big, bigger musicians.

## WPA—Federal Music Project

During the Great Depression, the Romani had yet another option: to perform their music as part of the WPA. President Franklin Roosevelt created programs to provide employment for many artists, writers, and musicians.

Specifically, "The prime objective of the Federal Music Project (1935–1939) and the subsequent WPA Music Program (1939–1943) was to give employment to professional musicians registered on the relief rolls. The project employed these musicians as instrumentalists, singers, concert performers, and teachers of music. The general purpose of the Music Project was to establish high standards of musicianship, to rehabilitate musicians by assisting them to become self-supporting, to retrain musicians, and to educate the public in the appreciation of musical opportunities."[35]

> In Detroit, two small bands—one made up of seven Serbs and Croats in a band called the Tamburitzans and the second an eight-member Hungarian Gypsy band called the Detroit Gypsy Orchestra—gave concerts throughout the city. Most of their shows took place in the area's hospitals, bringing "cheer to many who sorely need such a pleasant change of atmosphere," as the Detroit Federation of Musicians periodical said. The units also brought their ethnic music and folk instruments into the classrooms for discussion.[36]

Eleanor Roosevelt came to Detroit on November 14, 1940, to listen to music as part of the WPA programming. She was impressed with the music the Romanies were performing for people.

> I spent two of the pleasantest hours I have ever spent visiting music projects yesterday morning in Detroit. Churches have given space for rehearsal to these WPA units, so it was in the basement of a church that we listened to a gypsy band playing dance music, to which it was almost impossible to sit still.
>
> The leader has a delightful personality. They told me that when he plays in the schools, he tells the children stories of the gypsy customs. Last Christmastime he kept a group of youngsters enthralled while he told about the gypsy Christmas and played haunting gypsy music.[37]

### Romani Musicians' Versatility

These Romani musicians, whose ancestors had immigrated to the United States, performed in such a variety of venues in Michigan. Their versatility in playing different instruments, and their ability to adapt to the times and variety of environments in which they lived and in response to the demand for different kinds of music has been an amazing, ongoing journey. They have been and are truly resilient.

# The Romanies Today

Our musical culture is fading, partially because there are not a lot of opportunities for live music and musicians anymore and also because our people are meeting growing desires to excel in other fields.

—Lauren Slepsky-Chicko, vocalist

Over time, a variety of changes have occurred for the Romanies in Michigan—a few laws and ordinances have changed positively; while Romanies maintain close family ties, their musical culture has faded to some extent; and the United States Holocaust Memorial Museum has taken small steps to acknowledge their tragic history. While prejudice against them is still prevalent, a few glimmers of hope for positive change and awareness are evident. However, these hints of change still do not allow for a cohesive portrait of the Romanies in Michigan and their culture. They still remain out of sight in outlying Michigan communities. This situation begs for more research about this hidden, dispersed community and the importance of creating dialogue and trust with Romanies to learn more about them, their history, and their culture to help dissipate discrimination and racial profiling.

## Laws, Ordinances, and Changes

While Romanies usually no longer travel in wagons today in Michigan and elsewhere in the United States, and law enforcement agents are not literally shooing Romanies out of communities and the state today, newspapers and the police still warn the public about "Gypsy scams," another way of dispersing them from communities. Other articles talk about attempts to change laws that would limit or tax their activities. Positive, educational, and/or supportive articles about Romanies are scarce and/or nonexistent.

However, on a positive note, the American Civil Liberties Union (ACLU) advocates nationally for Romani rights and now oversees police activities related to Romanies and hate crimes. The Southern Poverty Law Center also monitors police activities related to Romanies and hate crimes throughout the United States. "We haven't collected any anti-Roma incidents since the election (2016) nor does it appear that we have any in our hate incident data base."[1]

A 2010 press release from the ACLU, "Maryland's High Court Strikes Down Montgomery County Fortunetelling Ban under First Amendment," hails a victory for Maryland but also speaks disparagingly of Warren, Michigan.

> BETHESDA June 10, 2010: The American Civil Liberties Union of Maryland hailed a decision by the Maryland Court of Appeals that strongly defends fundamental free speech rights in a case involving fortunetelling in Montgomery County (Maryland).
>
> In its decision, the state's highest court, in keeping with rulings from the Supreme Court and courts around the country, ruled that a Montgomery County ordinance banning fortunetelling is an unconstitutional restriction on protected speech.
>
> "This case has never been just about fortunetellers, but about the fundamental right to free speech," said Ajmel Quereshi, an attorney with the ACLU of Maryland. "While individual fortunetellers can be punished if they fraudulently exploit their customers, banning all fortunetelling is overbroad and unconstitutional. It is not the role of government to decide that broad categories of speech can be banned merely because it finds them distasteful or disagreeable."....
>
> Meanwhile, in Warren, Michigan, laws restricting fortune telling are

becoming stricter, while San Francisco has an outrageously convoluted licensing system for fortune tellers. Such laws have little to do with actually protecting people from fraud (anti-fraud laws do this adequately) and more to do with ameliorating complaints and protecting special interests.[2]

According to Eric Heimlich:

Some states and districts maintain policies and statutes that prohibit fortune-tellers, require them to pay hundreds of dollars for annual licenses, or otherwise control activities in which Gypsies engage. Despite the unconstitutionality of such measures, some rules apply specifically to Gypsies by name. . . . After a long history of avoidance of local authorities, Gypsies in the United States and elsewhere are becoming more politically active in defense of their civil and human rights; an international organization of Roma people has been recognized by the United Nations.[3]

Ian Hancock says, "It is a sad reflection on the state of justice in the United States, that, despite its unconstitutionality, Gypsies remain the only American ethnic minority against whom laws still operate, and who are specially named in those laws."[4]

*The Economist* reported, "At the end of last year (1998), a bill in New Jersey removed from the books the last law in the United States aimed at a particular ethnic group. The law, dating from 1917, allowed the state's towns to 'license and regulate roving bands of nomads, commonly called gypsies.'"[5]

However, Hancock says that county laws as well as state laws still exist. They are old, perhaps pre-1776, and seen as laws of the type "no riding a horse on Sunday"—only surfacing when they're looked for. It would take time and money to track them all down, and then get them rescinded.[6]

On another positive note, more recently, individuals and civil rights organizations have been challenging these discriminatory laws and practices. "Laws from the past still restrict those who see the future, but astrologers are successfully challenging the laws that inhibit their profession all across America. Four major court cases have been won, and dozens of cities have changed their laws on the 'occult.' The Association for Astrological Networking (AFAN) is committed to overturning every law that overly restricts the practice of astrology."[7]

In some Michigan communities, laws that discriminate against Romanies have been challenged and are changing. For many years, it was illegal in Michigan to tell fortunes for gain (charging a fee). PA 282 of 1993 revoked this prohibition, effective April 1, 1994. However, in Eastpointe and Kalamazoo, other changes have occurred.

> Apparently Eastpointe, MI, had a little problem with fake fortune tellers bilking citizens, so the city council passed an ordinance requiring psychics buy a $150 license to practice their craft.
>
> There's a new fortune telling ordinance in Macomb County. The Eastpointe city council finalized the ordinance protecting citizens from unscrupulous psychics. . . .
>
> To qualify for the license, which needs annual renewal, applicants must reveal any criminal background, operate within specific hours and fit the city's definition of a "fortune teller."
>
> That definition details quite extensively what qualifies as fortune telling, and lists acceptable tools, including crystals, coffee grinds and the occult, as well as proper usage of one's powers, which can be summoned for "effecting spells, charms, or incantations, or placing, or removing curses," among other things.[8]

In another community, the ACLU challenged a Kalamazoo ordinance, stipulating it was unconstitutional.

> Kalamazoo has an old ordinance that makes it illegal to engage in the business of "phrenology, palmistry, or the telling of fortunes." In December 2014, Kalamazoo police officers threatened to enforce this ordinance against Rev. Mark Hassett, a self-described spiritualist minister and practicing pagan, who was planning to perform a spiritual reading with a client at a local bookstore.
>
> The ACLU of Michigan wrote a letter to Kalamazoo officials warning that the ordinance is unconstitutional restriction of freedom of speech because the government has no business deciding which spiritual beliefs are "correct" and which are "fraudulent."
>
> The city attorney immediately responded and said he was instructing police not to enforce the ordinance, and that he would recommend that the

city repeal the ordinance in 2015. (ACLU Attorney Miriam Aukerman and Legal Fellow Marc Allen).[9]

## The Delray Community Fades

Sadly, the Hungarian-Slovak Romanies who once lived in Delray have dispersed. This thriving community and its vitality, with its music in the early to mid-twentieth century, has faded. During the 1960s, critical events occurred in Delray that forced thousands of ethnic Americans to begin to leave the community. Both external and internal factors of a cultural, economic, and transportation nature caused the Romani music community to disperse. However, documenting and preserving the memory of this amazing community is important.

First, Interstate 75 was constructed in 1964, which cut Delray off from Detroit, limiting people's mobility and ease to traverse the city.[10] After the 1967 Detroit uprising, many businesses moved to other communities. The intense factory pollution factor also pushed people out of the community.[11]

While many Romanies played the traditional Hungarian Romani music, over time, the number of musicians dramatically declined. Today, all the Romanies, along with many other ethnic groups, have left the Delray community. The Romanies migrated to Dearborn, Allen Park, Southgate, Wyandotte, and other suburbs, as well as Nevada and elsewhere, to perform jazz in bars and nightclubs, to pursue other careers, to retire, or to live close to other Romanies who had already left Delray.

The original Hungarian restaurants such as the Hungarian Village Restaurant, and bars such as Kovacs in Delray have since been demolished. The second Hungarian Village Restaurant in nearby Springwell was sold. As the demand for traditional Romani music began to disappear, many of these musicians adapted to the times and began to play jazz. Many of the younger people have also not wanted to carry on the tradition of learning to play the Romani music. Today, some Romanies still perform in different ethnic restaurants—Middle Eastern, Italian, Cuban, and others in the Dearborn area and downtown Detroit. Additionally, restaurateurs realized it was cheaper to have background recorded music in restaurants rather than hire live performers. On rare occasions, it is possible to hear Romani musicians perform their traditional music at specific events in Dearborn, Chicago, and Cleveland.

Construction is now underway for the Gordie Howe International Bridge, named after the late Canadian hockey player, which will be built between Windsor, Ontario, and Detroit, Michigan—more specifically Delray.[12]

While the Romani community from Delray is now dispersed, they still have strong bonds with one another and remain in close contact. They travel to each other's family celebrations, including weddings and funerals, both within Michigan and in different parts of the United States.

The Slepsky family, who once lived in Delray, moved to Dearborn along with most of the other members of the Romani community of Delray in the 1960s and 1970s. The community thrived in Dearborn during that time as well, up to the early 1990s. Many of the community that once lived in Dearborn and Delray have since moved to Las Vegas. Half of the Slepsky family now live in the Las Vegas area along with about half of the Roma community that had migrated from Michigan. They talked about the disappearing community of musicians, but still the importance of coming together for family celebrations. They, like other Romanies, mourn the loss of the vibrant music and community that once lived close together.

Lauren Slepsky-Chicko talked about the disappearing Gypsy music community.

I grew up seeing a lot of our grandparents' and parents' generations and remember them visiting each other's homes very frequently, hearing our traditional Gypsy music, cooking the traditional Eastern European cuisine, attending large funerals with tons of musicians, huge weddings where people would have a great time and enjoyed lots of dancing to both traditional and more contemporary music. Even the older generation of women, after you'd have dinner at a wedding they'd begin the dancing by doing the Chardas—it's a dance they did in a circle—while a large number of traditional Gypsy musicians played their instruments. It was just very traditional and cultural, and I always thought it was so beautiful. Their generations grew up hearing our music being played constantly in their homes by musicians in their families. Their parents were first- or second-generation immigrants so it was normal then, that you heard that kind of music being played all the time. Most of my generation and my parents' generation even heard this music being played in our own homes. So, growing up, I always thought this was all going to be a part of our lives and culture forever. And then, as we got a little older, we started to see all of these things die out as the older generations passed on. And as we grew up, my generation watched most of our culture fade, in Dearborn and Las Vegas, as I have lived in both communities. Our musical culture is fading, partially because there are not a lot of opportunities for live music and musicians anymore and also because our people are meeting growing desires to excel in other fields. Most of our current generations of people chose to pursue professions and careers that were better able to meet financial obligations and allow for greater success and assimilation into American society.

## Chris Slepsky, Lauren's father, said,

My father (Billy Rose [stage name]) taught us how to play the American jazz standards when we were kids. We were playing music such as the *American Songbook* standards, jazz, Sinatra, etc., so we would be able to make a living playing music. My generation also learned Motown, Rhythm & Blues, Soul, Funk, and Latin Music, which were the popular music most of my generation grew up on. Therefore, we didn't learn traditional Hungarian Gypsy music when we were kids, because the popular music in society changed before our time. We didn't play the traditional instruments that my father's generation did and those before him, since the popular music of their time was different, and they had an audience for this type of music. I learned drums when I was a kid. My brother Tony played bass; my other brother, Gary, played guitar and sang. However, my oldest brother, Gary, who has recently passed away, did also learn to play the Hungarian cimbalom when he was very young, and our Gypsy music was still thriving. He was playing concerts with the older generation when he was only twelve years old! Other cultures of people used to love to hear our traditional music and would come to hear them perform, as well as seek out our musicians for their parties and entertainment. However, the audience and desire to hear the traditional music of that era in America just kind of died out. But in Europe, they still play our traditional Gypsy music, because they still have an audience to play it for. . . . The little kids are still learning to play. Our music is still played by many in Europe, and there are still many great traditional Gypsy musicians thriving there. But it's sad that it's dying here in America. After the last of my father's generation, it will be gone.

Lauren's grandfather, Billy Rose, also agreed.

> Our music is gone here. Nobody listens to it. There's nobody to play it for.
> We used to play when our people would get married; there would be many
> musicians playing as the bride would be processing out of the house and
> going to the church, playing by the church as the wedding party processed,
> or at funerals—the same thing. Many musicians would play at the funeral
> parlor for the deceased, and they would follow on the way to the church
> in a procession of musicians, and then on the way to the cemetery. They
> don't do this anymore because there is not anyone left to play our music.
> Nobody wants to play it. We would play many Hungarian parties, Jewish
> bar mitzvahs, and many other parties and weddings throughout Detroit
> because people loved the music during those times. I loved to play Hungar-
> ian music with the orchestra, the gypsy orchestra. I really loved it. No one
> wants to hear this music anymore, and many don't even know of it. Soon it
> will be gone forever.

## United States Holocaust Memorial Museum

On April 14, 1994, the United States Holocaust Memorial Museum held its
first commemoration of Romani victims. While the museum recognizes
them, Hancock points out that the museum has not gone far enough to
acknowledge the extent of the Nazi destruction of European Romanies and
does not have the word "Holocaust" in their Romani-related displays.

A few years ago, Victor Moise and his daughter Angelina Moise Mala-
vanda visited the United States Holocaust Museum in Washington, DC.
Angelina said,

> Going to the Holocaust Museum in Washington, DC, was emotional. It was
> enlightening to know that the Gypsies were recognized as well as with the
> Jewish community and other nationalities and religions and everything
> else.
>
> And we talked to some of the workers there and they said, "Do you know
> who was in the concentration camps because we can't get anyone to speak
> to us about their experiences because the Gypsies especially still in Europe
> are very hush-hush and you couldn't get a detailed analysis?" It's nice to

know that they recognized their deaths. None of them had any survival rate at all, 'cause those were all burned to the ground. A lot of the population at the time was diminished, unfortunately.

Exciting, to see that the whole world will see in writing that Gypsies do exist, and they have their own language, their own food, their own traditions. It's not a make-believe Disney movie. For my generation at least, the Internet's a big deal. To have all of that in writing, right there.

Victor then said, "This was the first time that she realized we were being acknowledged, accepted, by a national source giving legitimacy to what I had been telling her. And we were both emotionally saddened by what we saw and were elated—just seeing the history of the Gypsies being so focused on by this facility. That was a duality of an impact there. We were both like 'Ahh! I can't believe.'"

## Michigan's Holocaust Remembrance Day

Additionally, progress has been made in Michigan in recognizing and acknowledging the Romanies who were slaughtered in the Holocaust. Michigan has had a Holocaust Remembrance week for many years. While language in earlier resolutions referred to the Romanies as Gypsies, House Resolution No. 283 was passed to declare May 4, 2016, as Holocaust Remembrance Day in the State of Michigan and now refers to them as Romanies.[13]

## A Call for More Research

While change is very slow, as Romanies and civil rights organizations begin to stand up for their human and civil rights and bring new and more understanding of these people, we can hope for additional research and dialogue to create more compassion and respect for them in Michigan and elsewhere.

# Recipes

## Palacinky

Casey and Marilyn Kanalos shared this Romani recipe passed down through Casey's family.

| | |
|---|---|
| 3 eggs | 2 cups flour |
| pinch salt | ¼ cup butter for the pan |
| 3 tbsp. sugar | jam (I prefer apricot) |
| 2 cups milk | |

Beat together: eggs, salt, sugar, milk, and flour until smooth. Heat a frying pan, brush with butter. Pour in a thin layer of batter and spread by tilting the pan off the heat. Return to heat. Pancake must be very thin, almost translucent. Fry on both sides until golden brown. Spread with jam, roll up, and keep warm until served. Dust with powdered sugar. Serves 4–6.

Another filling I like is a cheese filling.

| | |
|---|---|
| 1 lb. cottage cheese | 1 tsp. vanilla |
| ¼ cup butter | ½ cup golden raisins |
| ½ cup sugar | 1 tbsp. milk |
| 2 eggs separated | |

Rub cheese through a sieve. Cream butter, sugar, and egg yolks. Add cheese, vanilla, and raisins. Blend well; if mixture is too thick, add milk. Fold in stiffly beaten egg whites. Place in palacinky, roll it up, and bake at 350° for 5 minutes. Enjoy.

Eleanor Margitza shared two of her favorite recipes:

## Cabbage Noodles

2 sticks of butter
1 lb. or 12 oz. bag of bow tie noodles
1 large or 2 medium heads of cabbage

Melt 1 stick of butter in large pot. Add cabbage, cook until light brown and transparent, stirring often, scraping bottom of the pot. Add cooked noodles to cabbage. While this is cooking, place 1 stick of butter in a saucepot and melt on low flame until dark brown and foamy. Pour over cabbage and noodles. Salt to taste.

## Paprika Potatoes

½ lb. bacon cut into small strips
1 small onion diced
½ green pepper diced
1 tsp. paprika
½ tsp. salt

Pinch of pepper
5 medium to large potatoes,
  diced or sliced
1 cup water

Fry bacon until crisp, then remove. Add diced onion and green pepper. Sauté for 5 minutes. Add paprika, salt, and pepper. Add potatoes and water; cook until potatoes are tender. Top with bacon pieces.

# Timeline of Laws and Injustices

1417   Germany issues first anti-Romanies law and forty-eight more during next three centuries.

1568   Pope Pius V banishes Romanies from the Holy Roman Church.

1633   Philip IV of Spain declares Romanies do not exist and that they are really Spanish and speak made-up, artificial language.

1721   Emperor Karl VI (Holy Roman Empire) calls for extermination of Romanies throughout his domain.

1740   All Romanies crossing into Bohemia are ordered killed.

1782   Two hundred Romanies are tortured and executed following false charges of cannibalism.

1871   Scholars in Germany write that Romanies are inferior human beings.

1920   Despite German laws that state that all people are equal, Romanies are forbidden in parks and public baths.

1935   Nuremberg Law restricts Romanies to protect German blood and honor.

1937   Romanies are designated second-class citizens in Germany, without civil rights.

1940s  German Nazis exterminate between 500,000 and 1,500,000 Romanies.[1]

# Romani Groups Who Live in the United States

The Vlax are two-thirds of the overall Romani American population; they descend from ancestors held in slavery in the Rumanian Principalities of Wallachia and Moldavia.

The Romanichals, Romichals, or English Travellers are physically indistinguishable from the general Anglo-American population; they maintain a strong sense of separateness from the non-Romanies.

The Bashalde (means musicians) or Hungarian-Slovak Roma came to American as part of late nineteenth-century immigration of non-Romanies from Central Europe.

The Xoraxane is an Islamic population, originating in Macedonia and surrounding areas of the Balkans, who settled in the Bronx and established two mosques.

The Russian/Serbian Lova descended from Russian Roma who fled to Yugoslavia during World War I and traveled back and forth into Hungary, intermarrying with Lova from there.

The New Wave Romanies include Romanies who represent many different European groups, all of whom came to North America in the late twentieth and early twenty-first centuries.[1]

# Timeline of Romani Migration to the New World and United States

| | |
|---|---|
| 1544 | England deports Romanies to the New World. |
| 1655 | England transports Romanies as slaves to English colonies of Barbados and Jamaica. |
| 1695 | England deports Romanies to Virginia and then to penal colonies in Georgia. |
| 1851 or 1852 | First Romanies (two brothers) arrive in New York City from England. |
| 1855–1885 | Balkan Romanies move en masse to United States. |
| 1880s | Romanies from Hungary and Slovakia go to Cleveland, Ohio; Braddock, Pennsylvania; and Youngstown, Ohio, and work in steel mills. |
| 1890s | Romanies emigrate from Serbia to New York in response to government restrictions on nomadism. |
| 1920s | Romanies come from Austro-Hungarian Empire to New York; Homestead and Braddock, Pennsylvania; Delray, Michigan; and Chicago. |
| 1930s | Romanies move from other parts of the United States to New York City to access relief programs. |
| 1940s | Romanies begin to migrate to Las Vegas, Nevada. |

| | |
|---|---|
| 1956 | More Romanies emigrate from Hungary to the United States after Hungarian Revolution. |
| 1960s | Romanies begin to leave Delray for Dearborn and suburbs after Detroit riots and increase in pollution. |
| 1970s–1980s | Muslim Romanies from Yugoslavia immigrate to the Bronx, New York. |
| 1990s | Attacks increase against Romanies in Eastern Europe; more Romanies go to New York City. |
| 2000–2018 | An estimated 20,000 to 1,000,000 Romanies live in the United States.[1] |

Appendix 5

# Interviews

Unless otherwise noted, the quoted material in this book comes from the following interviews. In many cases, I had follow-up telephone conversations and e-mail communications to clarify information.

Renee Andra Bandy, telephone interview, August 23, 2016

David Bryan, interview, March 12, 2016

Christine Bryan, e-mail correspondence

Don De Andre, telephone interview, March 3, 2016

Paul Gifford, interview, June 29, 2016, Flint, Michigan

Evelyn Horvath Hallup, interview, May 7, 2016, Dearborn, Michigan

Éva V. Huseby-Darvas, interview, June 17, 2016, Ann Arbor, Michigan

Casey "Geza" Kanalos, interview, June 9, 2016, Southgate, Michigan

Michael Kral, interview, May 21, 2018, Royal Oak, Michigan

Mandy and Kim Kramar, January 5, 2017, Charlotte, Michigan

Angeline Rosemarie M., interview

Angeline Moise Malavenda, interview, July 7, 2016, Plymouth, Michigan

Eleanor Margitza, telephone interview, December 8, 2016

Richard Margitza, telephone interview, December 11, 2016

Rick Margitza, telephone interview, December 11, 2016

Richard S. Martin, interview, July 27, 2016, Portage Michigan

Larry Merino, telephone interview, January 14, 2016

Elaine Horvath Moise, interview, June 10, 2016, Southgate, Michigan

Victor Moise, interviews, June 10, 2016, Southgate, Michigan; July 7, 2016,
    Plymouth, Michigan

Steve Piskor, interview, June 10, 2016, Dearborn, Michigan

Billy Rose (stage name for Bill Slepsky), interview, March 3, 2016, Dearborn
    Heights, Michigan

Alex Sagady Jr., telephone interview, December 14, 2016

Chris Slepsky, interview, March 3, 2016, Dearborn, Michigan

Lauren Slepsky-Chicko, interviews, March 3, 2016, Dearborn Heights,
    Michigan; May 7, 2016, Dearborn, Michigan

Robert Takacs, telephone interview, February 4, 2017

William Tyler White, interview, July 28, 2016, Bath, Michigan

# Notes

## Preface

1. "'Gadjé' is not a proper noun, it only means (any) people who are not Romani There are plenty of proper nouns in Romani, like *Nyamtso* (a German), *Frantzuso* (a Frenchman), and so on, but not *gadjé*. Remember *gadjé* is the plural; the singular (male) is *gadjo*, and (female) *gadji*." Ian Hancock, e-mail message to author, February 4, 2019.
2. Šani Rifati, "Without Prejudice and Stereotypes: Please Call Me Rom," *The Best of Habibi* 17, no. 2 (1998), http://thebestofhabibi.com/volume-17-no-2-fall-1998/call-me-rom.
3. Steve Balkin, e-mail message to author, January 21, 2016.
4. Chastity Pratt Dawsey, "Goodbye to Delray, the Detroit Enclave Residents Are Getting Paid to Leave," *Bridge: News and Analysis from the Center for Michigan*, March 8, 2018, https://www.bridgemi.com/detroit-journalism-cooperative/goodbye-delray-detroit-enclave-residents-are-getting-paid-leave.
5. Suzuko Morikawa, "Dynamics, Intricacy, and Multiplicity of Romani Identity in the United States," in *Emerging Voices: Experiences of Underrepresented Asian Americans*, ed. Huping Ling (New Brunswick, NJ: Rutgers University Press, 2008), 116.

## Who Are the Romanies?

1. Anne H. Sutherland, *Roma: Modern American Gypsies* (Long Grove, IL: Waveland Press, 2017), 13.

2. Ian Hancock, "Gypsies," in *Harvard Encyclopedia of American Ethnic Groups*, ed. Stephan Thernstrom (Cambridge, MA: Harvard University Press, 1980), 441.

3. Marlene Sway, *Familiar Strangers: Gypsy Life in America* (Urbana: University of Illinois Press, 1988), 45.

4. Yaron Matras, *I Met Lucky People: The Story of the Romani Gypsies* (London: Penguin Random House, 2014), 33–34.

5. Ian Hancock, *We Are the Romani People* (Hatfield, UK: University of Hertfordshire Press, 2002), 32. See appendix 2, "Timeline of Laws and Injustices., for additional injustices and atrocities.

6. Ibid.

7. Michael Dregni, *Gypsy Jazz: In Search of Django Reinhardt and the Soul of Gypsy Swing* (Oxford: Oxford University Press, 2008), 79.

8. Ian F. Hancock, "Roma [Gypsies]," *Handbook of Texas Online*, http://www.tshaonline.org/handbook/online/articles/pxrfh.

9. Dregni, *Gypsy Jazz*, 254. See appendix 3, "Romani Groups Who Live in the United States."

10. Irving Brown, *Gypsy Fires in America: A Narrative of Life among the Romanies of the United States and Canada* (New York: Harper, 1924).

11. *Copper News*, Calumet, December 4, 1907, in Dave Engel and Gerry Mantel, *Calumet: Copper Country Metropolis, 1898–1913* (Rudolph, WI: River City Memoirs, 2001), 127–28.

12. Sway, *Familiar Strangers*, 5.

13. Dregni, *Gypsy Jazz*, 250–51.

14. "Gypsies," in *Encyclopedia of Cleveland History* (Cleveland, OH: Case Western University, 1993–2015), https://case.edu/ech.

15. Marlene Sway, "Gypsies," In *Encyclopedia of Chicago* (Chicago: Chicago Historical Society, 2005), http://www.encyclopedia.chicagohistory.org.

16. Bill and Sue-on Hillman's Erbzine, http://www.erbzine.com.

17. Steve Piskor, *Gypsy Violins: Hungarian-Slovak Gypsies in America* (Cleveland, OH: Saroma, 2012), 76.

18. Sway, *Familiar Strangers*, 59–60.

19. Sutherland, *Roma: Modern American Gypsies*, 23.

20. Šani Rifati, "Without Prejudice and Stereotypes: Please Call Me Rom," *The*

*Best of Habibi* 17, no. 2 (1998), http://thebestofhabibi.com/volume-17-no-2-fall-1998/call-me-rom.

21. Celestine Bohlen, "Spanish Martyr Is First Gypsy Beatified by Catholic Church," *New York Times*, May 5, 1997.

22. Evan Heimlich, "Gypsy Americans," *Countries and Their Cultures*, https://www.everyculture.com/multi/Du-Ha/Gypsy-Americans.html.

23. Sutherland, *Roma: Modern American Gypsies*, 104.

24. During the course of my research, I contacted Pentecostal churches within Michigan and elsewhere in the United States seeking Romanies to interview but got no response. I also spoke with a pastor at the Holy Cross Church in Delray to try to get some history about the Romanies who had once attended that church, but he would or could not provide any information.

25. Larry Merino, "Gypsy Resistance" (PhD diss., Concordia Theological Seminary, 2005), xiv.

## Always Traveling

1. Yaron Matras, *I Met Lucky People: The Story of the Romani Gypsies* (London: Penguin Random House, 2014), 35–36.

2. Ryalla Duffy, *On the Move in a Gypsy Waggon: Aspects of Romany and Traveller Culture* (Blackwell, UK: Robert Dawson, 2007), 5.

3. Hristo Kyuchukov and Ian Hancock, *A History of the Romani People* (Honesdale, PA: Boyds Mills Press, 2005), 16.

4. "Canton," *Wayne County Review*, July 2, 1880.

5. "Gypsies in Town, Travel Right Through," *Escanaba Daily Press*, July 12, 1929, https://www.newspapers.com/clip/17375681/the_escanaba_daily_press.

6. Ian Hancock noted that "Gypsy Vanners" are a kind of horse. The people who sell them here in the United States aren't Romanies. The actual Romani word for a wagon is a *vurdon* (*vurdona* would be the plural). In different dialects it is pronounced *verdon*. Only the Romanichals (Romanies from/in the United Kingdom) call it a *vardo* or a *vawda*. Since these horses are rare these days, the word is used by Romanichals for an automobile.

7. History of the Gypsy Vanner, http://willowwindstable.net/history/.

8. Ian Hancock pointed out that David Bryan refers to himself as a "true Gypsy," while also saying that his parents are Welsh and Irish, and therefore not Romanies. Hancock noted that David, a Traveller, used the label "Gypsy"

loosely, referring to his way of life rather than to his ethnicity, still a common misapplication of the word even in law enforcement.

9. Roma Caravans, http://www.romacaravans.com.au/history.html.

10. Nina Patel, "Tiny House, Big Benefits: Freedom from a Mortgage and Worries— and Stuff," *Washington Post*, June 25, 2015.

11. Lisa Prevost, "Where Can You Park a Tiny Home?," *New York Times*, October 6, 2017.

### Prejudice and Romanies

1. David Mayal, *Gypsy Identities, 1500–2000: From Egipcyans and Moon-men to the Ethnic Romany* (New York: Routledge, 2004), 275, cited in Suzuko Morikawa, "Dynamics, Intricacy, and Multiplicity of Romani Identity in the United States," in *Emerging Voices: Experiences of Underrepresented Asian Americans*, ed. Huping Ling (New Brunswick, NJ: Rutgers University Press, 2008), 116.

2. Anne H. Sutherland, *Roma: Modern American Gypsies* (Prospect Heights, IL: Waveland Press, 2017), 47–48.

3. Karen Lindquist, Delta County Historical Park, e-mail to author, May 20, 2016. Courtesy of the Delta Township Historical Society, 1930s.

4. Sandra Ballman-Burke, "Gypsies: A Forgotten People," honors thesis, Western Michigan University, 1989, 71–72 (Western Michigan University Archives, Paper 1428).

5. Ian F. Hancock, *The Pariah Syndrome: An Account of Gypsy Slavery and Persecution* (Ann Arbor, MI: Karoma Publishers, Inc., 1987), 143–62.

6. Sutherland, *Roma*, 5.

7. Marlene Sway, *Familiar Strangers: Gypsy Life in America* (Urbana: University of Illinois Press, 1988), 5.

8. The following vignette reflects a rare exception. After I gave a talk about the Romani and other marginalized peoples of Michigan to a group of seniors at the Allen Street Neighborhood Center in Lansing in the spring of 2018, I asked people to share any thoughts or stories about the Romanies that they might have. One woman, probably in her seventies, said that she grew up on a farm outside Lansing. She remembered that Romanies used to camp in the fields nearby. They made furniture from birch trees, which her parents used to buy. Her mother also packed up leftover food and put it outside for them and others to eat.

9. Carol Silverman, *Romani Routes: Cultural Politics and Balkan Music in Diaspora* (Oxford: Oxford University Press, 2012), 8.

10. Ian Hancock, e-mail to author, February 1, 2016.

11. "Drive Gypsies from Village, Fowlerville Marshal Succeeds in Getting Rid of Objectionable Band," special to the *State Journal*, May 12, 1913.

12. "Gypsies in Town, Travel Right Through," *Escanaba Daily Press*, July 12, 1929, https://www.newspapers.com/newspage/34283276.

13. "Gypsies Turned Loose by Police, No Evidence," *Ironwood Daily Globe*, August 28, 1974, 13.

14. Sutherland, *Roma*, 33.

15. Ian Hancock and Dileep Karanth, ed., *Danger! Educated Gypsy: Selected Essays* (Hatfield, UK: University of Hertfordshire Press, 2010), 195–96.

16. G. Boughourian and Jose Alcantara, "Gypsy Fortune-Tellers and Your Community," *Police Chief* (June 1975): 71–74, cited in Hancock, *The Pariah Syndrome*, 111.

17. Patricia Chargon, "Spring Is the Season of Con Artist Schemes," *Detroit Free Press*, April 30, 1985, 3A and 7A.

18. Cynthia Roldan, "Who Are North Augusta's Irish Travelers?," *The State*, December 13, 2016, https://www.thestate.com/news/local/crime/article96051242.html.

19. Hancock, *The Pariah Syndrome*, 105–6; and Walter Weyrauch, "Oral Legal Traditions of Gypsies and Some American Equivalents," cited in Morikawa, "Dynamics, Intricacy, and Multiplicity of Romani Identity," 118.

20. Sway, *Familiar Strangers*, 38.

21. Hancock, *The Pariah Syndrome*, 106, quotes James Smart, "A Gypsy Can't Be a Gypsy without a Gypsy License," *Philadelphian Bulletin*, April 11, 1969.

22. Hancock, *The Pariah Syndrome*, 105, quotes Harold J. Logan, "Maryland Gypsy Laws," *Washington Post*, January 29, 1976.

23. Volume 3 of *The Compiled Laws of the State of Michigan, 1915*, compiled, arranged and annotated under Act 247 of 1913 and Act 232 of 1915, Act 38, 1913, p. 57, Eff. August 14.

24. "Nation in Brief: Anti-Fortunetelling Law Is Attacked," *Los Angeles Times*, November 4, 1993.

25. Chuck Parker, "Fortuneteller Says She's Found a Legal Way to Set Up Shop," *MLive*, November 22, 2009, https://www.mlive.com/news/kalamazoo/index.ssf/2009/11/fortuneteller_says_shes_found.html.

26. "Can't Feel Skulls to Learn Future," *Lansing State Journal*, April 22, 1930.

27. "A Court Battle over Fortune-telling Is in the Cards . . . Michigan Law: Banning Fortune Telling for Profit," *Detroit Free Press*, March 29, 1981, 1, 13.

28. Fred Bronson, "Billboard Celebrates 120th Anniversary: A Look Back at the Rich History," *Billboard* magazine, November 1, 2014, https://www.billboard.com.

29. "Carney Lingo, Carnival Slang," https://www.goodmagic.com.

30. "No Grifts, No Gypsies," *The Billboard*, The World's Foremost Amusement Weekly Announcements, April 16, 1949 (Bad Axe, MI), 85.

31. "No Drunks or Gypsies" *The Billboard* (Fowlerville and Crosswell, MI), July 22, 1950, 75.

32. "No Girl Shows, Flats or Gypsies," *The Billboard* (Reed City, MI), July 22, 1950, 75.

33. *The Billboard* (Mason, MI), August 13, 1955, 67.

34. "Indoor Vendor Space Application," Otsego County Fair Association, Gaylord, Michigan (2016), at http://otsegofair.wpengine.com/vendor-information.

### Romanies in Outlying Michigan

1. Ore-Ida Foods Incorporated History, http://www.fundinguniverse.com/company-histories/ore-ida-foods-incorporated-history.

2. *(Soo) Evening News*, August 13, 1909.

3. Daniel Truckey, director/curator of the Beaumier Upper Peninsula Heritage Center at Northern Michigan University, shared such a memory about growing up in Wakefield, Michigan; e-mail to author, February 28, 2017.

4. National Park Service, Oral History Project, Buckett, J. 3.27.02; excerpt from oral historian technician Jo Orion's interview with John and Eleanor Buckett on March 27, 2002 (Jo Orion works for the Keweenaw National Historical Park); attachment to e-mail from Jeremiah Mason, archivist, Lake Superior Collection Management Center, Keweenaw National Historical Park, Calumet, Michigan, to author, December 19, 2016.

5. *The Diaries of James Trelore Buckett, 1905–1908, Calumet, Michigan*, transcribed and annotated by Barbara Buckett Leary (self-pub., Calumet, MI, 2013), 92.

6. Dave Engel and Gerry Mantel, *Calumet: Copper Country Metropolis, 1898–1913* (Randolph, WI: River City Memoirs, 2002), 23, 113, 117, 154.

7. Carol Silverman, *Romani Routes, Cultural Politics and Balkan Music in Diaspora* (Oxford: Oxford University Press, 2012), 83–84.

8. Irving Brown, *Gypsy Fires in America: A Narrative of Life among the Romanies of the United States and Canada* (New York: Harper, 1924), 3.

9. Ibid.

10. Ibid., 59–80. See Irving Brown's *Gypsy Fires in America* for a more lengthy description.

11. "Benton Harbor and St. Joseph Michigan Memories," Facebook.

12. According to Ian Hancock, it should be noted that royalty does not exist among the Romanies. "In our language, the words for 'king' and 'queen' are thagar and thagarni. They are not applied to any role within Romani culture, but to non-Romani kings and queens. The word for a leader is a baro. One can imagine Roma coming into a town, and being approached by the locals, perhaps the police chief, who asks to speak to the leader. He'll ask the leader what is his title, and be told 'baro', which isn't English, or perhaps be told 'king' since from the Romani point of view that is the English word for the top person. It began as a translation problem, but was quickly romanticized because of the literary 'Gypsy' image. From a king, the jump to a queen and a princess is easy. But these are not Romani concepts." Julie Cantrell, "About the Roma: Are There Really Kings and Queens?," Julie's Journal, February 10, 2012, https://juliecantrell.wordpress.com/2012/02/10/about-the-roma-are-there-really-kings-and-queens/.

13. "Gypsies Are Grateful for City's Kindness, Public Invited to Queen's Funeral," *News Palladium*, Benton Harbor, September 1, 1953, 1, 13.

14. Ibid.

### Hungarian-Slovak Romani Music in Delray

1. Steve Piskor, *Gypsy Violins: Hungarian-Slovak Gypsies in America* (Cleveland, OH: Saroma, 2012), 1–6.

2. Éva V. Huseby-Darvas, *Hungarians in Michigan* (East Lansing: Michigan State University Press, 2003), 17–18.

3. *1989 Festival of Michigan Folk Life: Michigan State University Museum* (East Lansing: Michigan State University, 1989), 48.

4. Ian Hancock, e-mail to author, February 1, 2016.

5. Huseby-Darvas, *Hungarians in Michigan*, 24.

6. Éva V. Huseby-Darvas, e-mail message to author, November 12, 2017.

7. Marlene Sway, *Familiar Strangers: Gypsy Life in America* (Urbana: University of

Illinois, 1988), 9–10.

8.  Erdmann Doane Beynon, "The Gypsy in a Non-Gypsy Economy," *American Journal of Sociology* 42, no. 3 (1936): 364–69.

9.  Gene Scott, *Detroit Beginnings: Early Villages and Old Neighborhoods* (Detroit 300 Partners Program of the Detroit Retired City Employees Association, 2001), 27.

10. Suki Gershenhorn, "What about Delray? The Past and Future of Detroit's Forgotten Neighborhood," blog, *Huffpost*, December 9, 2012, https://www.huffingtonpost.com.

11. Carol Silverman, *Romani Routes, Cultural Politics and Balkan Music in Diaspora* (Oxford: Oxford University Press, 2012), 4.

12. Piskor, *Gypsy Violins*, 14–15.

13. *Encyclopedia Britannica* (online).

14. Paul M. Gifford, *The Hammered Dulcimer: A History (Lanham, MD: Scarecrow Press, 2001)*, 131–32.

15. Piskor, *Gypsy Violins*, 125–26.

16. Interviews from the Owen W. Bombard Interviews Series, Benson Ford Research Center, Dearborn, Michigan, Research.center@thehenryford.org (Accession 65, The Reminiscences of Eugene J. Farkas, Benson Ford Research Center, The Henry Ford, 333–43, interview conducted January 1954).

17. Ford R. (Ford Richardson) Bryan. *Beyond the Model: The Other Ventures of Henry Ford* (Detroit: Wayne State University Press, 1997), 91–92.

18. Huseby-Darvas, *Hungarians in Michigan*, 22.

19. Ibid.

20. Piskor, *Gypsy Violins*, 129.

21. MDOT Report, *Above-Ground Resources Survey*, vol. 1, *The Detroit River International Crossing Study* (Lansing: Michigan Department of Transportation, 2007), 3, 52.

22. Ibid., 1, 64.

23. Ann Mullen, "Small-Town Appeal," *(Detroit) Metro Times*, October 1, 2003, https://www.metrotimes.com.

24. Hasan Dudar, "Kovacs Bar in Detroit's Delray Neighborhood Demolished: 'End of an Era,'" *Detroit Free Press*, November 7, 2017.

25. James S. Pooler, "The Open Road: It's Lost Its Old Attraction for Many of Detroit's Gypsies," *Detroit Free Press*, April 8, 1951.

26. Piskor, *Gypsy Violins*, 27.

27. Ibid., 131.

28. https://recordoobscura.blogspot.com/2009/04/dreams-of-budapest.html.

29. Michael Dregni, *Gypsy Jazz: In Search of Django Reinhardt and the Soul of Gypsy Swing*, reprint (Oxford: Oxford University Press, 2010), 7.

30. Ibid., 252.

31. Ibid., 259–60.

32. Ibid., 261.

33. Patricia Montemurri, "Melodic Gypsy Folk Songs Console Violinist's Fans," *Detroit Free Press*, September 3, 1989.

34. Piskor, *Gypsy Violins*, 133.

35. The U.S. Work Projects Administration Federal Music Project [collection], Library of Congress, http://memory.loc.gov/diglib/ihas/loc.natlib.scdb.200033720/default.html.

36. Kenneth J. Bindas, *All of This Music Belongs to the Nation: The WPA's Federal Music Project and American Society, 1935–1939* (Knoxville: University of Tennessee Press, 1995), 102–4.

37. Eleanor Roosevelt, "My Day," November 14, 1940, *Eleanor Roosevelt Papers Digital Edition* (2017), https://www2.gwu.edu/~erpapers/myday.

## The Romanies Today

1. Alex Amend, Southern Poverty Law Center, e-mail to author, November 28, 2016.

2. "Maryland's High Court Strikes Down Montgomery County Fortunetelling Ban under First Amendment," American Civil Liberties Union, Bethesda, Maryland, June 10, 2010, https://www.aclu.org.

3. Evan Heimlich, "Gypsy Americans," *Countries and Their Cultures*, https://www.everyculture.com/multi/Du-Ha/Gypsy-Americans.html.

4. Ian Hancock, *The Pariah Syndrome: An Account of Gypsy Slavery and Persecution* (Ann Arbor, MI: Karoma Publishers, Inc., 1987), 105.

5. "From Open Road to Internet," *The Economist*, March 26, 1998.

6. Ian Hancock, e-mail to author, July 3, 2018.

7. Jayj Jacobs, "The Law and Astrology," Association for Astrological Networking, Beverly Hills, CA, November 6, 1994, https://www.afan.org.

8. Andrew Belonsky, "Eastpointe Puts New Fortune Telling Ordinance into Effect," WXYZ (Eastpointe, MI), March 22, 2011.

9. ACLU attorney Miriam Aukerman and legal fellow Marc Allen, "The Right to Predict the Future: American Civil Liberties Union of Michigan," ACLU Michigan, December 18, 2014, http://www.aclumich.org/article/right-predict-future.

10. M. A. Maidenberg, "Delray: The Determined Struggle of a Village Condemned to Die," *Detroit Free Press*, May 11, 1969, 4B.

11. Danielle Trauth-Jurman, "The Story of Delray: A Case Study on Environmental and Restorative Justice in Detroit," honors project, Bowling Green State University, ScholarWorks@BGSU, May 5, 2014, 124.

12. Joe Guillen, "Blight Removal Targets Detroit's Delray Neighborhood," *Detroit Free Press*, November 24, 2015.

13. Michigan Legislature, House Resolution 0283 (2016), http://www.legislature.mi.gov/doc.aspx?2016-HR-0283.

### Appendix 2. Timeline of Laws and Injustices

1. Ian Hancock, *We Are the Romani People* (Hatfield, UK: University of Hertfordshire Press, 2002), 32–37.

### Appendix 3. Romani Groups Who Live in the United States

1. Ian Hancock and Dileep Karanth, eds., *Danger! Educated Gypsy: Selected Essays* (Hatfield, UK: University of Hertfordshire Press, 2010), 129–31.

### Appendix 4. Timeline of Romani Migration to the New World and United States

1. Ian Hancock, "Gypsies," *Harvard Encyclopedia of American Ethnic Groups*, ed. Stephan Thernstrom (Cambridge, MA: Harvard University Press, 1980), 441; Rena Gropper, *Gypsies in the City: Culture Patterns and Survival* (New York: Darwin, 1975); Ian Hancock, *The Pariah Syndrome: An Account of Gypsy Slavery and Persecution* (Ann Arbor, MI: Karoma, 1987); *The Encyclopedia of New York City*, 2nd ed., ed. Kenneth T. Jackson (New Haven: Yale University Press/New York Historical Society, 2010), 563; Steve Piskor, *Gypsy Violins: Hungarian-Slovak Gypsies in America* (Cleveland, OH: Saroma, 2012), 4.

# Resources

**Michigan State University**

Lockwood Collection of Romani Ethnology and Gypsy Stereotypes, Special Collection, Michigan State University Libraries

*https://lib.msu.edu/spc/romani/*

The late Professor Emeritus William G. Lockwood began collecting material about the Romanies in the late 1950s, gathering scholarly works and documents, Roma music and poetry, and representations of Gypsies in the arts and popular culture. The collection includes several thousand books and periodicals, twenty boxes of vinyl albums, and several hundred examples of sheet music. The William G. Lockwood Collection of Romani Ethnology and Gypsy Stereotypes is as geographically diverse as the Romanies themselves, with publications from Europe, Asia, Africa, and the Americas. The collection will be an outstanding resource for students and scholars who are researching stereotypes of Gypsies.

The William G. Lockwood Romani Music Collection

*https://www.discogs.com/lists/MSU-Libraries-William-G-Lockwood-Romani-Music-Collection/281361/*

This Romani music collection is a subset of the larger William G. Lockwood Collection of Romani Ethnology and Gypsy Stereotypes that was donated to Michigan State University Libraries. These musical recordings date from 1912 to 1998. **95**

## G. Robert Vincent Voice Library

*https://lib.msu.edu/vvl/*

The Michigan State University Libraries will house the oral history interview recordings and transcriptions of interviews I conducted for this book, as well as my research notes.

## Michigan State University Museum

*http://traditionalarts.msu.edu/resources/collections/collection/?kid=A2-33F-25*

The Gus Horvath collection at the Michigan State University Museum includes Gus's last cimbalom, made in Hungary and embellished by him, which the museum acquired in 2000 with the support of the Hungarian Art Club of Dearborn and the MSU Office of Vice-President for Research and Graduate Studies. Other donations include copies of his photo albums and scrapbooks, sheet music, bills of sale for musical instruments, tools, and equipment. Gus used to embellish his instruments, copies of photographs, handbills, newspaper clippings. All of the materials highlight Gus Horvath's long musical career and provide context to augment our understanding of Gus's instruments, of Gus, and of the community of musicians.

## Other Institutions in Michigan

### Benson Ford Research Center, The Henry Ford, Dearborn, Michigan

Photographs and documentation including interviews from the Owen W. Bombard Interviews Series, Benson Ford Research Center, Dearborn, Michigan.

### University of Michigan Collection, Romani Studies

*http://guides.lib.umich.edu/c.php?g=282921&p=1885236/*

## Other Institutions in the United States

### Romani Archives and Documentation Center, University of Texas at Austin

According to the website for the Department of Linguistics, "The Romani Archives and Documentation Center is the largest collection of items documenting the Romani people and culture in the world. It consists of over 25,000 books, monographs, bound articles, papers and letters, prints, transparencies, photographs, audio- and video-recorded material, framed and unframed prints and documents as well as many other non-media items."

United States Holocaust Memorial Museum

*https://www.ushmm.org*

Archive materials include photographs, video clips, and oral histories of Romanies from Europe.

The Smithsonian

*http://www.smithsonianeducation.org/migrations/gyp/gypstart.html*

### Organizations

European Academic Network on Romani Studies

*http://romanistudies.eu*

Gypsy Lore Society

*http://www.gypsyloresociety.org*

### Movies, Videos

*American Gypsy: A Stranger in Everybody's Land,* dir. Jasmine Dellal, 1999.

*Latcho Drom,* dir. Tony Gatlif, 1993.

*Tales of a Gypsy Caravan: When the Road Bends,* dir. Jasmine Dellal, 2007.

*Song of the Dunes: Search for the Original Gypsies,* dir. Paula Fouce and William Haugse, 2009.

*A People Uncounted: The Untold Story of the Roma,* dir. Aaron Yeger, 2011.

*King of the Gypsies,* dir. Frank Pierson, 1978.

### Online

Steve Balkin, "Romani (Gypsy) Culture on the Internet, blog, Roosevelt University, https://blogs.roosevelt.edu/sbalkin/roma/

# For Further Reference

Acton, Thomas. *Gypsies*. Morristown, NJ: Silver Burdett, 1982.

———. *Gypsy Politics and Traveller Identity*. Hatfield, UK: University of Hertfordshire Press, 1997.

Ballman-Burke, Sandra. "Gypsies: A Forgotten People." Honors thesis, Western Michigan University, 1989.

"Barry A. Fisher: Attorney and Human Rights Advocate." *Freedom Magazine* https://www.freedommag.org/english/vol29i4/page36.htm.

Beynon, Erdmann Doane. "The Gypsy in a Non-Gypsy Economy." *American Journal of Sociology* 42, no. 3 (November 1936): 358–70.

Bindas, Kenneth J. *All of This Music Belongs to the Nation: The WPA's Federal Music Project and American Society, 1935–1939*. Knoxville: University of Tennessee Press, 1995.

Brown, Irving Henry. *Gypsy Fires in America: A Narrative of Life among the Romanies of the United States and Canada*. New York: Harper, 1924.

Bryan, Ford R. (Ford Richardson). *Beyond the Model: The Other Ventures of Henry Ford*. Detroit: Wayne State University Press, 1997.

Buckett, James Trelore. *The Diaries of James Trelore Buckett, 1905–1908, Calumet, Michigan*. Transcribed and annotated by Barbara Buckett Leary (Self-published, Calumet, MI, 2013).

Dregni, Michael. *Gypsy Jazz: In Search of Django Reinhardt and the Soul of Gypsy*

*Swing*. Reprint. Oxford: Oxford University Press, 2010.

Duffy, Ryalla. *On the Move in a Gypsy Waggon: Aspects of Romany and Traveller Culture*. Blackwell, UK: Robert Dawson, 2007.

Engel, Dave, and Gerry Mantel. *Calumet: Copper Country Metropolis, 1898–1913*. Randolph, WI: River City Memoirs, 2001.

Fonseca, Isabel. *Bury Me Standing: The Gypsies and Their Journey*. New York: Random House, 1996.

Fraser, Angus. *The Gypsies*. Cambridge: Wiley-Blackwell, 1992.

Gifford, Paul M. *The Hammered Dulcimer: A History*. Lanham, MD: Scarecrow Press, 2001.

Gropper, Rena. *Gypsies in the City: Culture Patterns and Survival*. New York: Darwin, 1975.

Hancock, Ian F. "The Consequences of Anti-Gypsy Racism in Europe." *Other Voices* 2, no. 1 (February 2000), http://www.othervoices.org/2.1/hancock/roma.html.

———. "Gypsies." In *Harvard Encyclopedia of Ethnic Groups*, edited by Stephan Thernstrom. Cambridge, MA: Harvard University Press, 1980.

———. *The Pariah Syndrome: An Account of Gypsy Slavery and Persecution*. Ann Arbor, MI: Karoma Publishers, Inc., 1987.

———. "Roma [Gypsies]." *Handbook of Texas Online*. http://www.tshaonline.org/handbook/online/articles/pxrfh.

———. *We Are the Romani People: Ame Sam le Rromane Džene*. Hatfield, UK: University of Hertfordshire Press, 2002.

Hancock, Ian F., and Siobhan Dowd, eds. *The Roads of the Roma: A PEN Anthology of Gypsy Writers*. Hatfield, UK: University of Hertfordshire Press, 1998.

Hancock, Ian F., and Dileep Karanth, eds. *Danger! Educated Gypsy: Selected Essays*. Hatfield, UK: University of Hertfordshire Press, 2010.

Huseby-Darvas, Éva V. *Hungarians in Michigan*. East Lansing: Michigan State University Press, 2003.

———. (Veronika Huseby). "Ethnic Radio: A Study of Hungarian Radio Programs in Detroit and Windsor." *Michigan Discussions in Anthropology*, no. 7, special issue, "Beyond Ethnic Boundaries" (1984).

Kyuchukov, Hristo, and Ian Hancock. *A History of the Romani People*. Honesdale, PA: Boyds Mills Press, 2005.

Lewis, David Lanier. *The Public Image of Henry Ford: An American Folk Hero and His Company*. Detroit: Wayne State University Press, 1976.

Ling, Huping, ed. *Emerging Voices: Experiences of Underrepresented Asian*

*Americans.* New Brunswick, NJ: Rutgers University Press, 2008.

Liszt, Franz. *The Gypsy in Music.* Vols. 1–2. London: W. Reeves, 1926.

Lockwood, William G., and Sheila Shalo. *Gypsies and Travelers in North America: An Annotated Bibliography.* (Publication No. 6). Cheverly, MD: Gypsy Lore Society, 1994.

Matras, Yaron. *I Met Lucky People: The Story of the Romani Gypsies.* London: Penguin Random House, 2014.

Mayal, David. *Gypsy Identities, 1500–2000: From Egipcyans and Moon-men to the Ethnic Romany* (New York: Routledge, 2004).

Merino, Larry. "Gypsy Resistance." PhD dissertation, Concordia Theological Seminary, 2005.

———. *No Word for Love.* Fort Wayne, IN: Couragio Press, 2014.

Miller, Carol. *The Church of Cheese: Gypsy Ritual in the American Heyday.* Boston: GemmaMedia, 2010.

Nemeth, David. *The Gypsy-American: An Ethnographic Study.* Lewiston, NY: E. Mellen Press, 2002.

Oprea, Alexandra. "Psychic Charlatans, Roving Shoplifters, and Traveling Con Artists: Notes on a Fraudulent Identity." *Berkeley Journal of Gender, Law & Justice* 22, no. 1 (2007): 31–41.

Piskor, Steve. *Gypsy Violins: Hungarian-Slovak Gypsies in America.* Cleveland, OH: Saroma, 2012.

"The Reminiscences of Eugene J. Farkas." Owen W. Bombard Interviews Series, Benson Ford Research Center, The Henry Ford, Accession 65, pp. 333–43, Dearborn, MI, 1954.

Rifati, Šani. "Without Prejudice and Stereotypes: Please Call Me Rom." *The Best of Habibi* 17, no. 2 (1998), http://thebestofhabibi.com/volume-17-no-2-fall-1998/call-me-rom.

Silverman, Carol. *Romani Routes: Cultural Politics and Balkan Music in Diaspora.* Oxford: Oxford University Press, 2012.

Sutherland, Anne H. *Gypsies: The Hidden Americans.* Long Grove, IL: Waveland Press, 1986.

———. *Roma: Modern American Gypsies.* Prospect Heights, IL: Waveland Press, 2017.

Sway, Marlene. *Familiar Strangers: Gypsy Life in America.* Urbana: University of Illinois, 1988.

———. "Gypsies." In *The Encyclopedia of Chicago*, edited by James R. Grossman,

Ann Durkin Keating, and Janice L. Reiff, 371. Chicago: University of Chicago Press, 2004.

Takacs, Robert. "Growing up in Delray." Old Delray. http://www.old-delray.com/ GrowingUpInDelray-Takacs.htm.

Trauth-Jurman, Danielle. "The Story of Delray: A Case Study on Environmental and Restorative Justice in Detroit." Honors project, Honors College, Bowling Green State University, ScholarWorks@BGSU, May 5, 2014.

Velez, Alexi M. *The Roma Uncovered: Deconstructing the (Mis)Representations of a Culture.* Master's thesis, Florida Atlantic University, 2012.

Vinyard, JoEllen. *For Faith and Fortune: The Education of Catholic Immigrants in Detroit, 1805–1925.* Chicago: University of Chicago Press, 1998.

Weyrauch, Walter O. *Gypsy Law, Romani Legal Traditions and Culture.* Berkeley: University of California Press, 2001.

Yoors, Jan. *Crossing: A Journal of Survival and Resistance in World War II.* Prospect Heights, IL: Waveland Press, 1988.

———. *The Gypsies.* New York: Simon and Schuster, 1967.

———. *The Heroic Present: Life among the Gypsies.* New York: Monacelli Press, 2004.

Zuber, Pamela M. "Boon or Boondoggle? The WPA in the United States and Michigan." Master's thesis, Oakland University, 2003.

# Index